Design Secrets:
Architectural Interiors
50 Real-Life Projects Uncovered

GLOUCESTER MASSACHUSETTS

ROCKPORT PUBLISHERS

Justin Henderson/Nora Richter Greer

First published in the
United States of America
by Rockport Publishers, Inc.
33 Commercial Street
Gloucester, Massachusetts 01930-5089
Telephone: (978) 282-9590
Facsimile: (978) 283-2742
www.rockpub.com

ISBN 1-56496-576-7

10 9 8 7 6 5 4 3 2 1

Design: Leeann Leftwich

Cover Design: Madison Design &
                Advertising, Inc.

Cover Photo: Björg Amarsdottir (Tow Studios)

Printed in China.

contents

ways of creating interiors

By Rysia Suchecka

The vital processes of design go far beyond the apparent stillness of the final photo.

Putting in order the glimpses of intuition, the sketches, technical drawings, emotions, disappointments, and gratifications serves as a conscious point of departure, providing a metabolic surge...a moving on...to uncharted territory, with one consciousness. Not for form in itself, which is not the final purpose of our work, but for the result! There is no beginning and there is no end; flux, which by its nature is becoming, cannot be stopped.

The single stable reference is what was found, and is the nexus of our work; to search...to seek the very sense, perhaps, of our lives.

So, how do you accomplish the aesthetic sign that can deliver or move the observer?

To master the skill of the process of interior design, is to have the ability to organize, but to act as an artist, freely, heeding only the urgencies of one's need of expression. But artifice in an interior and its décor cannot and must not be the copy of an authentic ancient structure, nor the modern version of any historic style. Nor even an attempt to interpret the past. It is a work that is as far as possible, authentic and relevant!

The Components for Planning an Interior Are:

- The urgency behind one's own research for the project.
- The wish to realize the client/owner's dream, discovering the right blend of atmosphere and function.
- Creating a sense of "belonging" in a place—not necessarily resembling either the interior space or the building holding it, but rather bringing in the pieces of images from the outside—the view, the square, and its monuments, the genius loci...and melding everything—furniture, souvenirs, collections, works of art, dreams, expectations, energy, types of work—to the story of who will use it and/or live there. Making an intelligent reality.
- The concept of two dimensions to build elements that mark separate space, or divide it.
- Design with understanding of the trinomial: man, space, and nature.
- Understand the language of the time—we must capture the eternal aspect of a moment. We must respond to changes, exploring fashion, music, art, and technology of our time. This gives us a sense of the times outside interior architecture and design. If you do architecture and/or interiors, and you are not involved in your time, in the music of your time, the art, fashion, and technology of your time, you can not speak the language of your time. Designers must be able to speak the language of their time, because interior architecture is a public art, and our responsibility is to link life with art. If we are to build a human and connective interior architecture that has resonance, we must capture the eternal aspect of a moment.

Whatever we design must be of use, but at the same time transcend its use. It must be rooted in time, site, and client need, and yet it must transcend time, site, and client need.

process revealed

By Justin Henderson

A beautiful and functional interior does not spring full-blown from the forehead of its creator like the offspring of a god, soaring down from Olympus to land in the streets and then in the pages of a coffee table book. It is instead the end result of a lot of hard, often messy and exacting work accomplished by driven, talented people. That work takes place long before the photographs are taken, in the studios and conference rooms of design firms and their clients, in airports and planes and restaurants and hotel rooms all over the world, as plans are made and finalized; and then on the job site, when the project is built and the interiors finished. This book offers evidence of that work, the process of design.

Admirers of fine architecture and design have seen and loved countless coffee table books filled with pretty pictures of buildings and interiors—and this book offers its share, for no design book feels complete without a generous selection of glamorous photos. But given the glut of books filled with such perfect images, we decided to take a different approach here. In an effort to reveal something more about how these 50 interiors—ranging in scale from multiple floors in an office high-rise to a single, meticulously detailed staircase—got made, we asked designers to give us, along with the usual beautifully composed photographs, some of the nitty gritty: sections, drawings, sketches, scrawls, notes, anything and everything two-dimensional that might help reveal the process of design.

The response from the 30 firms whose 50 projects are featured in the book was mixed. While most of these architects and designers are media-savvy, many are not used to revealing the working materials—the behind the scenes, back of house stuff—that goes into their projects. And so, while a number of designers gave us everything we asked for and more, others claimed to have thrown the stuff out, or archived it in impossible-to-reach storage cabinets, or misplaced it and didn't have time to search. Others simply refused to give us background material on the grounds that these working images were not pretty enough, or refined enough, or finished enough, for publication.

But that was the point! we responded. To reveal the struggle, the real work, behind the design. Process is not always pretty (although there are plenty of compelling drawings here). And in the end, this talented group of designers and architects provided us with a wealth of samples of the many kinds of images generated en route from concept to construction to completion. The images range from elegant watercolors to CAD-generated perspectives to photos of models to mundane, detail-heavy construction documents. Some were done for marketing purposes, to sell ideas to clients, or to give clients a sense of what to expect; others were created during in-house brainstorming sessions, as design teams worked their way towards conceptual clarity or finished product. Fed by software-savvy designers, computers generated many of these images, while others may have been scrawled on cocktail napkins over late night drinks or during one of the countless flights hardworking designers take, en route from one project to another. A number of them were made for contractors, so they could see how the light fixture attached to the ceiling or how the window fitted into the wall.

Whatever their source or original purpose, in the context of this book, accompanied by narrative texts and photographs of the finished projects, these images help reveal some of the ways designers do their work. In this book, secrets of the design process are yours to savor and decipher.

bobo residence

TOM KUNDIG, OLSON SUNDBERG KUNDIG ALLEN ARCHITECTS, WITH JANICE VIEKMAN AND DAVID GULASSA
Seattle, Washington

Seen from the street or entrance side, the house presents layered concrete walls, highlighted by the cupola over the front door, but offers little evidence of the wide open drama occurring on the other side. Curving rooflines soften the rectilinear massing. The house was inserted into the midst of existing gardens created over the decades by the previous owner of the property.

Although this minimalist steel, concrete, and glass studio/residence at first glance seems at odds with the woodsy, organic style commonly associated with the Northwest, photographer/artist Carol Bobo's house has deep roots in its Seattle location. The inclusion of a wall saved from the original house on the site—a postwar brick rambler torn down to make way for the new house—literally links new with old, and the new owner with the former owner, a close personal friend. At the same time, the view-embracing sweeps of glass, the landscape-saving integration of the building into the site on a bluff overlooking Puget Sound, and the use of tough, honest materials, all resonate with the Northwest tradition—as does architect Tom Kundig's commitment to the principles of green design. Today, concrete and steel are more cost-effective and "earth-friendly" than wood, once the region's primary building material—and its primary industry.

The Bobo house emerged from a potent creative collaboration. "The process of collaboration is never easy," says Kundig, "but it is always gratifying. And Carol's house is a project that feels complete because the collaborative effort was so successful. Usually people pay lip service to the idea of collaboration, but Carol was different. She was passionate about the house, and she knew she was the driving force behind the project—yet at the same time she trusted everyone, and paid atten-

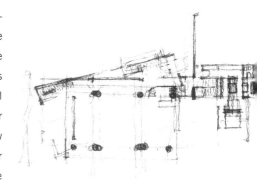

Early site plan, with existing wall—the skewed line at top—already integrated into the new building. Faint traces of the old house show the shift in axis. Primary structural support posts are represented by the dark circles.

Drawing of the new cupola over the entry set atop the old wall.

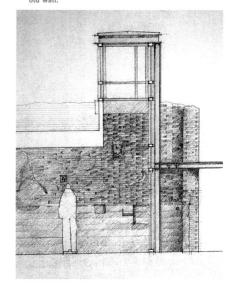

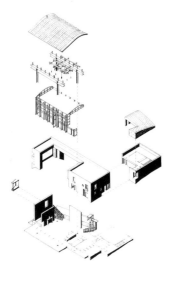

An early version of the house, in model form.

Exploded axon shows the various components of the structure.

Views of the cupola/entry illustrate how it bridges the space between the remnant wall of the original house on the site, at right, and the new house to the left. The skewed angle of the old wall relative to the new building creates the quirky V-shape of the entry.

Views from the southwest and west show the integration of the house into the existing landscape. The west-facing wall of the main living space is composed of glass framed in unfinished, unpainted steel, with a tall pivoting glass door providing access to the patio and gardens. Supported on steel posts and a massive steel beam, the lead clad copper roof extends outwards to shelter the patio.

tion." The conceptual "team" initially included Kundig, Bobo, and interior designer Janice Viekman; later, industrial designer David Gulassa and his crew made a significant contribution, as did many of the tradespeople, notes Kundig: "Trades people are not always trained to be aesthetes, but they know their work and their materials so well they work from the heart."

For Kundig, the primary means of communication with his visually oriented client was drawing; he made countless sketches and drawings. A few are reproduced here, to illustrate some of the ideas that emerged from the collaboration. As is evident in comparing drawings with photographs, some made it into the design; others didn't.

The house has been sited on the same spot as the previous one, but rotated to a more orthogonal westerly axis to improve the views. As a result, the fragment of wall from the original house is skewed off-grid. As one approaches the entry, the original wall angling across appears to open the door of the new home, creating a sense of passage from old into new—an "aha!" moment of "poetic juxtaposition" that happened strictly by accident, according to Kundig.

A custom-designed steel fireplace and an Aubusson carpet add richness to the living area at the north end of the Big Room. Scrims help diffuse the sunlight pouring in through the glass wall.

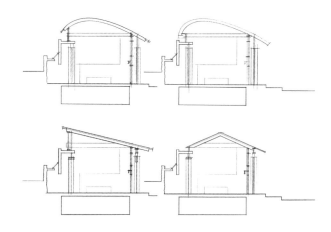

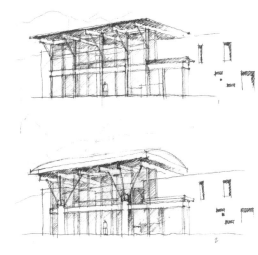

⊗ Studies for different roofs, in flat and three-dimensional perspective.

⊗ A tall pivoting glass and steel door links the dining area of the Big Room to the patio on the west side of the residence. White-painted "booties" add a touch of whimsy to the table legs.

⊗ The roof extension and the massive beam provide shelter and screen the sun. Pivoting door provides access to the exterior deck.

The structure's street façade consists of imposing layers of solid concrete walls, highlighted by a lantern-like cupola over the front door. The large, gridded steel door, set off by the old brick wall, leads into the vast, powerful volume of "The Big Room." Open from end to end, this 26-foot-high (7.8-meter-high), 52-foot-long (15.6 meter-long), and 33-foot-wide (9.9 meter-wide) steel-framed central volume serves several purposes: kitchen, dining room, living room, and photo studio. To the west a wall made of glass-framed-in-steel to form a Mondrian-like composition offers sweeping views of Puget Sound (layers of scrim can be dropped to screen out the western sun and control light in the studio). A varnished plaster ceiling arcs overhead (the arched roof is made of lead-coated copper), extending outside to the west to shelter the window wall. Inside, a steel grid suspended from the ceiling holds theater lights and a dozen spotlights made from bud vases. A pair of caged fans helps control the heat rising from the radiant concrete floors, as does a tall, pivoting glass door integrated into the glass wall. The floors have been intentionally left unsealed; like the rusting steel and the concrete walls,

⊗ Interior of the Big Room's east wall from the west, with figures to show scale.

they remain in their natural state, and will bear the traces of passing time, footprints and candle wax, water stains, even scribbles from the manufacturer and the installer. "Carol has a strong sense of materials in time," says Kundig, "she appreciates eroded concrete and rusted steel."

At one end, an enormous concrete-topped steel island defines the open kitchen, with a pull-out concrete-topped table built-in underneath. Behind the kitchen's back wall lies a utility core, containing pantry, powder room, and laundry area. In the center of The Big Room, the dining area includes a grouping of custom teak tables designed by Bobo and Viekman with special finishes by Gulassa. A massive sculpted candelabra by Gulassa hangs overhead. White-painted "booties" on the table legs add a touch of whimsy. The tables ride on casters for mobility; remember, the space was also conceived as a photo studio. At the other end, a spare yet comfortably furnished living room area features a steel fireplace designed by Kundig and fabricated by Gulassa.

The Big Room is flanked by a pair of wings; the north wing contains a pair of offices, while the south wing shelters the bedrooms and the caretaker's quarters. The bedrooms for Bobo and her teenage daughter are relatively small—"cave-like refuge spaces" in contrast with the immensity of the Big Room. Yet each has been designed and furnished with the same passionate intensity brought to every inch of the building—an intensity perhaps belied by the look of rusted steel and eroding concrete walls.

Industrial-strength stairs link the Big Room with upper level offices at the north end, bedrooms at the south. This north end stair lies on axis with the old wall from the original house.

For all the concrete and steel, the house's unique bathrooms offer wonderfully inviting, user-friendly spaces, with sculpted cabinets, exposed plumbing, warm finishes, and, in the master bath, great views from a soaking tub set into a window.

Site plan with existing pool and gardens surround the new house. The big room and terrace lie beneath the large rectangle; the garage is at bottom right. The old wall angles into the building; the widest point of the angle is the entry and front door.

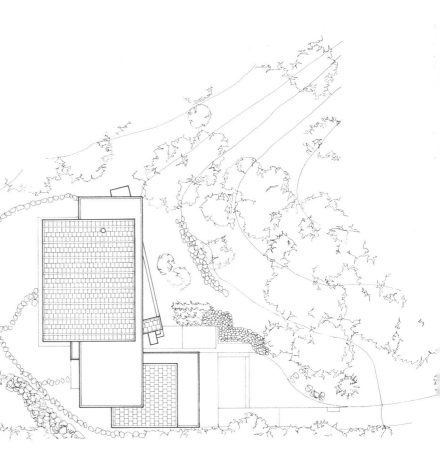

atherton residence

ARCHITECTURE BY OLSON SUNDBERG KUNDIG ALLEN ARCHITECTS; INTERIOR DESIGN BY TERRY HUNZIKER

Atherton, California

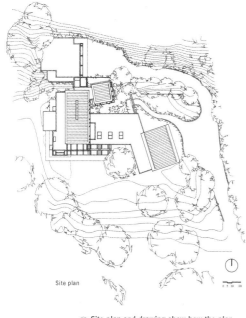

Site plan

Site plan and drawing show how the plan and scale of the house make it fit harmoniously into the existing, well-established landscape.

This design process began with the demolition of the house the owners had occupied on the spacious, lushly planted site for 30 years. They raised a family there, and raised a garden as well. In commissioning the design for a new house from Olson/Sundberg Architects, the owners requested that the gardens be left undisturbed: that the new house be integrated into the landscape as the old was. In a sense, the site was home; the challenge to the architects was to make a new house that would not lose that sense of place.

In researching the kind of house they desired, the owners had investigated Japanese architecture, and found the perfect example of what they sought in the Katsura Palace in Tokyo, a building renowned for the way its spare, graceful architecture blends harmoniously with the gardens that surround it. Jim Olson's design for the house looks nothing like the Katsura Palace—except that subtle echoes of the palace can be found in the way the house serenely blends into the established, 30-year-old gardens. The new house sits on the edge of the site's wooded area, opening out onto a spacious lawn, thus linking two environments—shelter and opening. Like the site, the house offers both a sense of refuge or shelter, and a viewpoint, a place from which to see the terrain—and to be part of it.

With the demolition of the old house, Olson began sketching impressions of the new house, with interiors and exteriors envisioned as one, woven into the landscape. In creating the new structure Olson absorbed input from both halves of the client couple. The husband, an engineer, requested that the house express an appreciation of technology—and that it be able to withstand the most severe possible earthquakes—no trivial matter in the land of the San Andreas Fault. The wife was more interested in finishes and textures, asking that the designers use subtle, natural materials, like those used in Japanese temples. Together, husband and wife are avid art collectors, with a taste for artworks made of

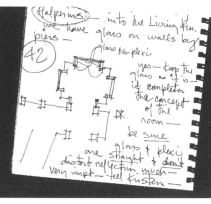

Pages from architect Jim Olson's notebooks show early concepts for the floor plan, rooflines, and other elements.

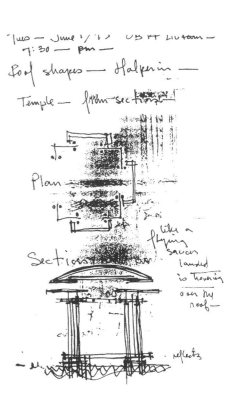

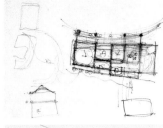

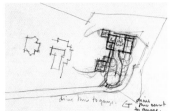

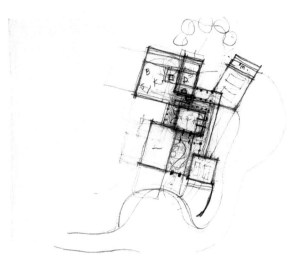

natural materials, like wood and stone, preferably left in their original state. The house is constructed of these natural materials, complementing the artworks—and the gardens.

To accommodate the artworks, the floor plan provides a number of gallery-scale spaces, counterpointed by more intimate living areas—three conceptual areas, representing different aspects of life. The first area is the Nest, including the kitchen and family room downstairs, and bedrooms upstairs in the house's main wing. The Nest focuses on providing the essential comforts of residential living. The second area is the Garden, here consisting of the formal dining room and the gallery areas on the lower floors. These sections of the house are deeply linked to the outdoors, with doors that open to connect the interiors with adjacent gardens. The third area is the Temple, evoked by the serene, light-filled space of the formal living room, a separate wing set at an angle, and connected to the main building via a light-filled gallery passageway.

The materials used inside carry over to the surrounding patios and outdoor spaces, erasing the division between inside and out, letting them flow together and bring the gardens into the house; for example, wooden pillars have been used for structural support. By connecting the pillars to floor and beams with steel braces, the designers lend them a weightless, floating quality, furthering the sense that the house rests gently, unobtrusively on the site. The house's walls and sliding doors are in many cases made of glass, enhancing transparency, and allow-

⊗ The evolution of the site and floor plan through numerous early drafts shows how the architects worked with the existing landscape, trying different configurations on the way to the realized plan.

⊙ An early version of the final floor plan.

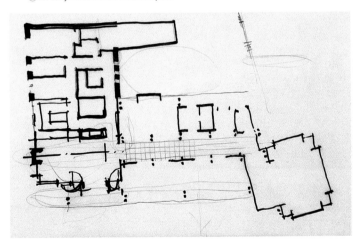

⊘ Exploded isometrics reveal the layered components of the house.

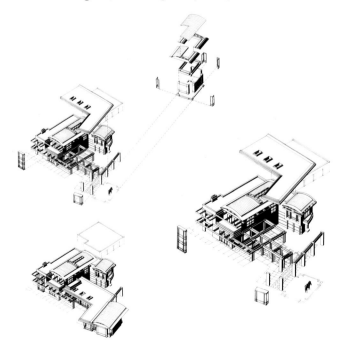

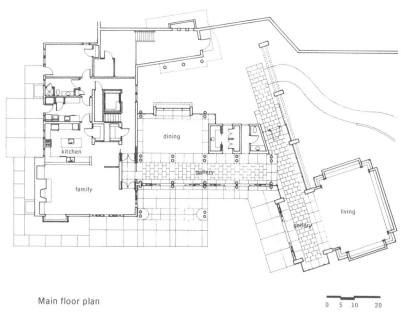

Main floor plan

0 5 10   20

⊘ Main floor plan shows the living quarters "Nest" at left, including family room and kitchen on this level, the "Garden" at center, including the dining room and galleries, and the "Temple" or living room at far right.

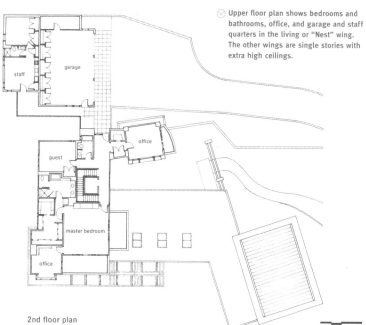

⊘ Upper floor plan shows bedrooms and bathrooms, office, and garage and staff quarters in the living or "Nest" wing. The other wings are single stories with extra high ceilings.

2nd floor plan

0 5 10   20

⊗ The family room features an installation by artist Andy Goldsworthy, consisting of myriad small sculptures made of leaves and twigs, each placed in its own niche in a wooden frame flanked by window walls.

⊗ The house is divided into three conceptual zones; two are shown here: the two-story wing at left is the Nest, containing the living quarters—kitchen and family room, downstairs, and bedrooms upstairs. At center and right, the Garden contains the formal dining room and galleries.

Decks and trellises create the connections between interior and exterior.

Dominated by an elegantly rusting metal horse created by artist Deborah Butterfield, the house's living room is an essay in serenity, with a beautifully lit domed ceiling transforming the space into the Temple, the third conceptual zone of the house. All the furniture was custom-designed by Terry Hunziker.

By placing glass inserts beneath the house's curving stainless steel roof, the designers lend the roof a weightless quality, making it seem as if it is floating over the house.

View of the dining room and galleries, which together form the conceptual space of The Garden, illustrate the transparency of the building envelope, allowing a powerful visual connection of interior and exterior, of house and surrounding gardens.

ing views through the house that visually unite the building with the landscape. The effect is deepened by the glass inserted beneath the house's curving stainless steel roofs, for it makes the roof appear to float, suspended above the building.

Furnished with custom-designed pieces by Terry Hunziker, the oversized ground-floor spaces provide dramatic backdrops for the owners' artworks, including large-sized pieces like the Deborah Butterfield horse, a bulky yet elegant assemblage of rusting metal standing calmly in the living room. The big rooms with their direct connections to the surrounding gardens also make great spaces for entertaining large numbers of people. Yet the essential quality of the house is a sense of calmness or serenity. The living room (the temple) features a domed ceiling, positioned as if floating above stainless steel soffits, with natural light flowing in through windows screened by translucent, glare-diffusing plexiglass.

In the Nest area the traditional creature comforts of the kitchen, family, and bedroom are warmed with darker background colors, though plentiful daylight still washes in from the generously scaled windows. The family room offers the visual highlight of an installation by Scottish artist Andy Goldsworthy. In keeping with the natural materials bent of the entire house, the piece consists of a group of small, shapely sculptures made from dried and compressed leaves and twigs. The evocatively shaped pieces occupy a tall wooden frame, with each placed in an individual, appropriately scaled niche. The whole work is set against a solid wall flanked by floor-to-ceiling glass, offering a fascinating study in different ways of "framing" natural compositions. The nearby kitchen, also finished in warm colors, offers the things that make kitchens work: plenty of counter and storage space, a central island, and practical materials including stainless steel and an acoustic tile ceiling to keep sound from the rest of the house. The upstairs master suite features a curved ceiling that lends it greater height and spatial drama, and a garden-view balcony to further the sense that house and site are one.

kuhling/wilcox residence

FOUGERON ARCHITECTURE

Palo Alto, California

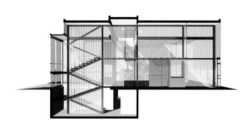

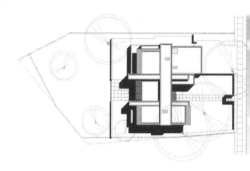

Elevations show various views of the house, an elegantly balanced composition of horizontal and vertical elements in steel, stone, and glass. The black stripe is the polished granite entry passage. The stair tower is enclosed in clear glass, with panels of channel glass slicing through its center.

Located in the Silicon Valley town of Palo Alto, California, the Kuhling/Wilcox residence offers 5,000 square feet (450 square meters) of thoughtfully orchestrated modern residential space, elegantly fitted into the relatively small footprint of an undistinguished 1960s suburban rancho. The original intent was to remodel, but the old house kept getting in the way, and so it was razed to make way for the new. The designers stayed within the existing footprint, however, to avoid complications with plan approval and also to leave intact the gardens designed by landscape architect Topher Delaney, who introduced the property's owners to project architect Anne Fougeron (this was her first residential commission). In the end, the back garden was saved while the front yard was redesigned around the new house—a stunning, richly finished composition primarily made of steel, stone, and glass. (Given the penchant of Palo Alto's *nouveau riche* for building lot-line to lot-line *faux chateau,* and the city's belated attempts to control these grandiose urges, it took two years to get plans approved anyway.)

The intent was to build monumentally, and lastingly, without making a structure that depended on traditional notions of "monumentality." In other words, build big

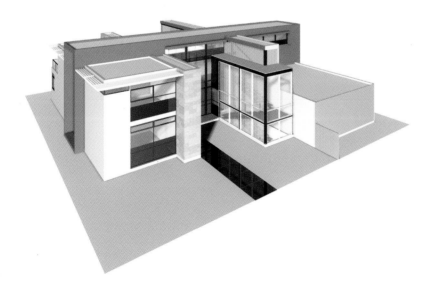

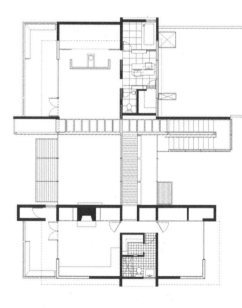

Floor and site plans show how the large house fits onto its small lot, and illustrate the distribution of space over two floors. The house's two blocky wings abut the central family room.

This view includes the entry seen from inside, right, the bridge linking the two parts of the second story, top right, and the stair tower at left. A translucent screen of channel glass slices up the middle of the stair. Wooden book and display shelves lining the bridge add warmth upstairs; a rich wood floor achieves a similar effect in the circulation spine at left.

A limestone fireplace creates a focal area in the soaring volume of the double-height living room; classic modern seating in red and white complements a glass-topped table set on a floor of polished black granite.

A view of the family room from the kitchen area.

without referencing the palace or chateau. While 5,000 square feet (450 square meters) on two stories qualifies as a fairly large house, what lends an opulent quality to the building are the surface finishes: on the exterior, polished granite and French limestone, steel, endless walls of glass, and cedar. Interior finishes also include hand-rubbed plaster, pear wood, steel-fronted cabinets, and a hardwood called garrah. These finishes and textures were developed, notes Fougeron, with full-scale mock-ups to allow the designers and clients to test and experience every surface.

When creating the interiors the design team hid all the connections, keeping the busyness to the minimum to hold the focus on the materials. The result is a modernist's dream: nothing there but the wonderfully rich and varied surfaces and the inside/outside spaces, ranging from intimate to soaring, that the surfaces enclose and embrace. Fougeron grew up in Paris, and this house subtly evokes a Paris landmark: Pierre Chareau's Maison Verre, from 1929, one of the classics of the Modern movement. Fougeron may be an admirer of Chareau and the classic Modernists, but she's a resolutely contemporary architect, and so the Kuhling/Wilcox residence also integrates intriguing contemporary materials, such as the 10-inch (25 millimeter) wide, English-made channel glass, that were unavailable in Chareau's time.

A view into the dining area across the circulation spine; the translucent channel glass wall meets the bridge at top. Wood floors and hand-finished plaster walls add richness to the cool, modern spaces.

A view across the living room takes in the dining area at left, and the bridge at upper right, with a row of wooden bookshelves lining one side. The channel glass wall slides through the staircase at right, and allows light in while maintaining privacy on the upper level at top left.

The two-story house is laid out with two rectangular wings abutting a central, double-height open family room flanked by a glass-enclosed circulation spine (including a sculpted stair tower) on one side and a limestone clad storage wall on the other. One wing contains the living room, graced with an open kitchen and dining area in the same volume. A bedroom and a deck occupy the second story over the living room. Across the central family room, the other wing houses an office and guestroom on the ground floor, and a second office and an exercise room upstairs. A bridge spans the family room above the front entrance, linking the separate upper level areas.

With two-story high, channel glass walls encasing the circulation spine, window walls supported by narrow steel columns, and frosted glass floors resting atop narrow beams, the building is virtually transparent, a layered and tiered glass box positioned between the front and back gardens. A black granite swatch laid down the middle enhances the connection, forming the entry passage in front, the family room floor inside, and a patio in the back. Similarly, the slatted ceiling extends outside to form trellised canopies. The landscaped gardens

With a pair of basins separated by a steel cabinet, the bathroom offers the cool luxury of fine materials: white marble, Panama granite, woven metal, and glass.

A translucent glass floor and glass walls line the upstairs walkway leading into the glass stair tower.

Wooden bookshelves double as display boxes lining one side of the upstairs bridge.

Another view from the bridge offers a view down into the living room. Glass walls and panels everywhere permit maximum transparency and light flow.

offer a few surprises, such as the "rocks" made from melted windshields with embedded fiber optics to make them glow in the dark. The furnishings palette balances contemporary pieces with modern classics in quiet tones—with an occasional flare of bright color thrown in for a highlight.

The opulent materials and the dynamic interplay of horizontal and vertical planes, counterpointed by the slashing diagonals of the stairs, lend the house a visual richness that surprises and delights—particularly given the essentially spare, unadorned quality of the structure. This is a monumental building, rich in materials and textures, happily lacking the pretense of historical baggage but graced with the staying power of great design.

woods residence

STEVEN EHRLICH ARCHITECTS

Santa Monica, California

This clean, rectilinear modern house perches on the side of a chaparral-covered bluff in Santa Monica Canyon, affording commanding views of the Pacific Ocean and the Malibu Mountains. So satisfying is the image that is hard to visualize the transformation that has taken place here. The house was originally designed and built in 1975. Ten years later, a remodel changed the building with the addition of a 650-square-foot (58.5-square-meter) deck. More recently architect Steven Ehrlich was commissioned to expand the house by approximately one-third in size and completely gut and remodel the interior, primarily with the purpose of strengthening the connection between inside and outside.

Ehrlich began with a complete demolition, saving only the staircase, and turning the interior into an empty shell. To initiate the transformation, Ehrlich created pockets for the kitchen's sliding doors, thus "evaporating" the barrier between interior and exterior.

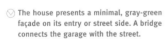
The house presents a minimal, gray-green façade on its entry or street side. A bridge connects the garage with the street.

Early drawings show how Ehrlich viewed the building as open, with a "porous façade" extending into the landscape on one side, and closed, facing the street, on the other. The elevation drawing includes the aluminum panels that contain masses, or volumes, that extend out from the building and house functional components like storage and/or counters.

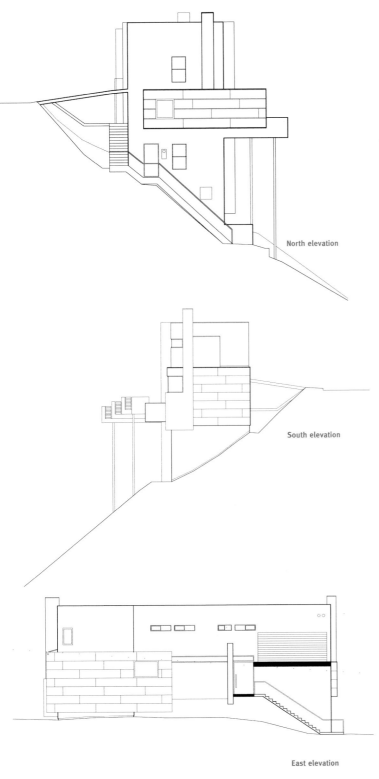

North elevation

West elevation.

South elevation

Ehrlich added a new wing with a deck, and stepped it back from the existing building to remain consistent with the stepped rhythm that already defined the building. It also allowed the living and dining room corners to be glazed, maximizing ocean views. The new wing is also 2 feet (0.6 meters) lower than the existing house, which means the new living room has a higher ceiling and thus a more generous spatial quality.

New elements have been added to the exterior skin. Clad in aluminum panels, these elements are attached to the main cubic form of the primary stucco structure, and then painted a gray-green color. In addition to creating interesting, contrasting new structural volumes on the exterior, they serve functional purposes, housing work counters or storage spaces that support the principal spaces to which they are attached. Two fireplaces, one at each end of the house, also serve as massing elements. Finished in a burnished gray concrete stucco, these fireplaces add more cubic forms to the composition.

Spare yet rich, and suffused with light, this serenely minimal composition offers a wonderfully satisfying interplay of inside and outside. For all the functional toughness of the materials—concrete, glass, aluminum, limestone, and wood flooring—the elegantly composed structure is remarkably user-friendly.

East elevation

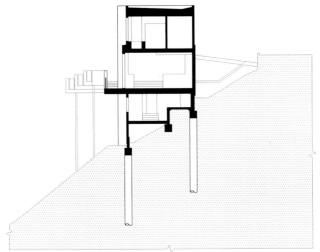

Cross section

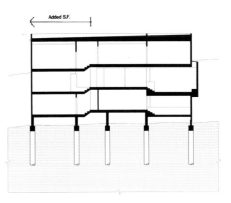

Added S.F.

Longitudinal section

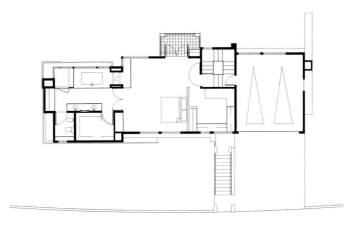

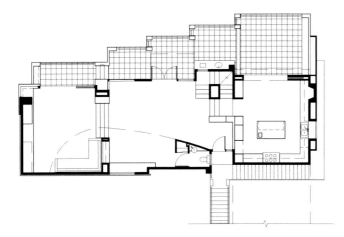

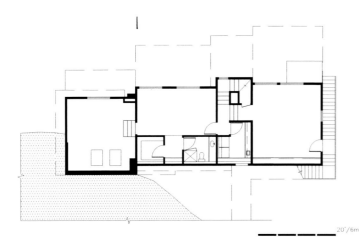

⌃ Third, second, and first floors, from top. The new wing lies at far left.

20'/6m

⌃ Expansive decks grace the northwest-facing view side of the house; the new wing, (above), is
⌄ slightly lower than the existing sections of the house. By slightly setting back the new wing, the architect made room for wraparound glazing on the corner.

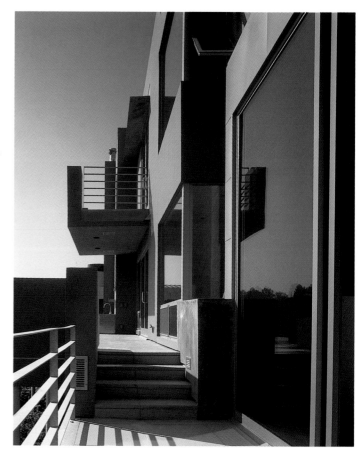

The kitchen and an adjacent terrace are connected by sliding doors that disappear into pockets, evaporating the barrier between inside and outside. Wooden floors and cabinetry warm the minimal, rectilinear interiors.

Generous expanses of glass on the west flood the house with daylight. The cubist, minimalist interiors are softened with a soothing, intriguing interplay of refined materials—wood, stucco, stone, steel, glass—well-chosen artworks and furnishings, and the counterpoint of transparency, translucency, and opacity.

alessio residence

IVAN RIJAVEC ARCHITECT

Australia

Images of the exterior and interior illustrate the unusual, geometrical forms that shape the Alessio House. For all the voluptuous curves and challenging forms, the house looks quite user-friendly and comfortable.

Ivan Rijavec, working away *Down Under,* practices architecture with an intellectual intensity that puts most architects to shame. And yet far from being an academic, exploring his theoretical fancies in the safe setting of Unbuilt University, Rijavec runs a thriving practice, building everything from institutional complexes to art galleries, and a number of strikingly original residences as well. The Alessio House, shown here, is a "typical" Rijavec house in that it expresses some of the more radical ramifications of geometry in architecture—for this is Rijavec's chosen field of exploration. As he has written: "Our projects begin with the simplest resolution of the brief into a graphic, which through the various stages of the design process is transmuted by way of numerous adjustments of curvature and incline, into geometries that render the perceiver conscious of the subjectivity of our cognitive system...the motive is to place the viewer into a natural...quandary of perception.... Thus a tango of surprise ensues, between the perceiver's vision, their imagination, and the architecture that is the subject of their perception."

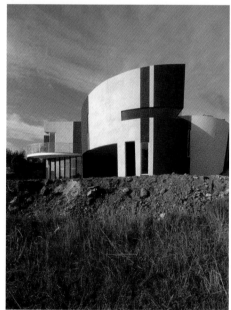

The Alessio House is a typical Rijavec house in that it expresses some of the more radical ramifications of geometry in architecture.

It sounds as if Rijavec is attempting to push the limits of architecture into the realm of surrealism. To do so while making functioning buildings stands as a remarkable feat—one that the designer has repeatedly accomplished.

The computer plays a large part in Rijavec's work: "The computer's role in the exploration of these geometries has paved the way for an objectification of the design process...resulting in an acceleration of the development of ideas. The tangled multitude of various curves can be represented on different layers and switched off when the composite representation becomes illegibly dense.... The effectiveness of this way of working has rendered the pencil more or less obsolete on some of our most recent projects."

The computer plays a large part in Rijavec's work. The pencil has become more or less obsolete in his most recent projects.

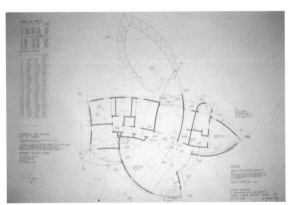

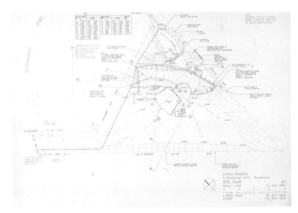

And thus the stage is set. Rijavec's philosophy is too complex to be explicated in so few words, or illustrated with a single project. But have a look at the Alessio House, a quintessential Rijavec project—original, distinct, and exotically appealing. Included are images of the house, inside and out, and a series of photographs taken during construction.

According to the architect, "The role of internal focus in this house is assumed by a conical kitchen, which in its glossy, vertically striped black and white finish, straddles the intersection of the living, dining, and family spaces, these folding outwardly like the blades of a Swiss Army knife." The plan reveals this aspect. The photographs show a house that breaks all the rectilinear rules, yet manages to be comfortable, stylish, and graceful.

Construction photos show the process of building this unusually shaped house is perhaps more complicated but fundamentally the same as constructing a more typically rectilinear building, with a wooden frame serving as the primary structural element.

These photographs show a design that breaks all the rectilinear rules, yet manages to be comfortable, stylish, and graceful.

pennsylvania farmhouse

DRYSDALE DESIGN INC.

Lancaster County, Pennsylvania

The small farmhouse is surrounded by gently landscaped gardens.

The light-filled living room had previously been two dark rooms. Furnishings are pared-down to allow appreciation of the "understated architecture," including the sawn-hewn ceiling and pine floor.

Private getaways unmask much of our hidden selves, and how a designer meticulously pieced her country home together reveals vast secrets about her thought process. Such is the case with Mary Douglas Drysdale and the renovation of a mid-eighteenth century farmhouse located in Lancaster County, Pennsylvania. Her holistic approach reflects her Renaissance training in architecture, interior design, and industrial design.

Drysdale started with a small, dark antiquated farmhouse. Her first objective was understanding the origins of the Amish-influenced house—i.e., placing its design on an historical timeline. The year 1823 was carved into the jamb above the front door, but "judging from the construction and plan of the house, I decided it was built fifty to seventy-five years earlier and that the jamb had been added later," Drysdale commented. She immersed herself in the historic design and then worked on a "contemporary reinterpretation of the style."

She soon realized that the original floor plans would be inadequate for modern living. Originally, the first floor was two cramped rooms. Drysdale reconfigured this space into one larger room and expanded it to include a sophisticated galley kitchen. Yet, she retained the bare pine floors, adding new flooring where necessary, and maintained the rough simplicity of the hand-hewn beams, which are actually the second floor joints. The entire second floor was converted to a single room, save a small bathroom (without shower). The third floor (attic) became a combination guestroom and den.

Stencils were taken from historical patterns.

View through the dining room and living room to the front door.

In addition to the interior architecture, Drysdale decorated the entire farmhouse, including the folk motifs, such as the cow seen from the dining room.

An Amish quilt matches the canopy around the bed.

For Drysdale, this underlying plan was most fundamental. "It must be rational and comfortable," she said. "It begins with the relationship of the grounds to the house, moves on to how the rooms relate to each other, and only then do you come to how one piece of furniture connects to another.... No matter how expensive the pieces, if the plan isn't comprehensive, the room will fall short of its potential. A good plan allows even humble materials to shine."

Once this plan was established, Drysdale delighted in adding an aged patina to the interiors and in decorating the house with a mixture of Amish and nineteenth century Philadelphian antiques. (She chose pieces from Philadelphia as some settlers migrated to the area from the big city). Exposed beams were dry-brushed with five coats of white pigment for a textured effect. New pine floors on the main floor were washed yellow, gray, and orange and columns antiqued with a crackled finish. Stenciling in the master bedroom was copied from eighteenth century designs. Fabric and furniture decoration

⊗ Bathing takes place in a copper tub in the bedroom.

⊗ A cozy nook in the attic.

⊗ One of Drysdale's many folk motifs.

⊗ Millwork takes on an added importance in the kitchen.

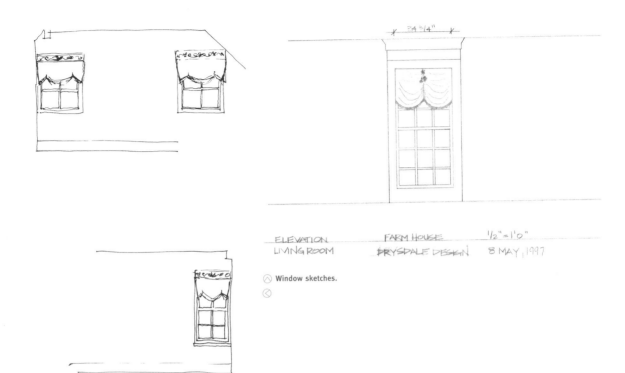

ELEVATION   FARM HOUSE   1/2"=1'0"
LIVING ROOM   DRYSDALE DESIGN   8 MAY, 1997

⊗ Window sketches.

was the next layer, including Amish hooked rugs, Amish quilts, fancy fabrics, fine-painted nineteenth century Baltimore chairs. Yet, Drysdale didn't forget modern amenities. If you look closely, you'll find a big-screen TV (hidden in a cabinet) and a sub-zero refrigerator.

From the exterior, the farm house is a quiet, simple place. Inside, however, it is a charming retreat, filled with a gentle mix of folk history, unusual antiques, and warm intentions.

⊗ A sketch of the sitting alcove.

emerald hill road residence

WOHA DESIGNS (WONG MUN SUMM AND RICHARD HASSELL)

Singapore

A view of the house from the main road shows the cleaned up but otherwise unchanged façade and pitched tile roof. The traditional Singapore shop houses are never more than 19.8 feet (6 meters) wide.

The house shown here in Singapore's Emerald Hill Historic District (after construction but prior to the specification and installation of furniture and fixtures) was a dilapidated wreck when purchased by a young professional couple planning to turn it into a stylish urban home. Yet its reconstruction was strictly controlled, particularly regarding the exterior. The solution was to create a new form set inside the existing volume.

In 1989 the Emerald Hill Historic District, off Orchard Road, became one of the first neighborhoods in the city/state to earn historic preservation status. Consisting primarily of two-story terrace houses in a range of design styles spanning 90 years, Emerald Hill had by 1989 degenerated to the point where it was assumed that complete demolition and redevelopment were inevitable. Instead, the district was preserved, with great success: Emerald Hill today stands as one of Singapore's most exclusive neighborhoods, a quiet residential enclave just a few yards from the bustle of Orchard Road.

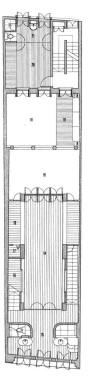

First and second story plans.

Roof and attic story plans.

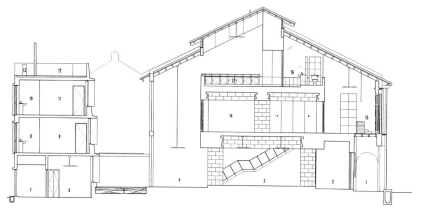

Longitudinal section across swimming pool.

Looking back at the elevated living room, and the master suite above, from the dining room. The street façade is visible beyond the wood floored living room.

View across the living room toward the courtyard and the rear block housing the kitchen and the guest quarters. The stairs run up between the newly inserted sandstone box and the original building wall, of rough brick that has been painted to contrast with the smooth new box.

According to Richard Hassell of WoHa Designs, the structure chosen for renovation is a Late Terrace House Style shop house, built in the 1920s. The façade and roofline had to maintain scale and appearance in keeping with the street. The interiors and rear façade were less strictly controlled, however, to allow for differing layouts and the installation of modern facilities. The rules allowed designers to replace the rear block of the building, which housed kitchen and bath functions, as long as the new structure did not go higher than the existing main roof eaves.

Singapore shop houses traditionally appear small from the street, for the front elevations are usually less than 19.8-feet (6 meters) wide. But the buildings are deep, stretching back 66 or 99 feet (20 or 30 meters) from the street, covered with a high pitched roof that creates a volume up to 49.5 feet (15 meters) in height—with unfortunately little access to light and air. In renovating such structures, Hassell notes, "There is a wonderful moment when the floors are removed and the entire space is revealed—the rough brick party walls catching the light streaming in between the broken roof tiles—a space inherent in the form, but usually concealed with partitions and floors. The traditional shop houses, although creating lively and vibrant streetscapes, provided dark and unremarkable internal spaces." The WoHa designers decided to create "an internal experience equal in impact to the external appearance."

Wood and white walls make an appealing contrast in the high-ceilinged master bath, located in the upper level of the new box.

View from a window overlooking the small courtyard that lies between the front and back buildings.

A view across the courtyard into the triple height dining room. Beyond the glass wall and the dining room, the living room and the master suite are stacked in the newly inserted box.

To this end they created a new form set inside the existing volume. The new volume is a sandstone box, sitting free of the old walls. Narrow stairs run between the old and new, "dramatizing" the tall, narrow volume. The new sandstone box divides the ground floor, with a raised living area located between the foyer and the dining area. Above, the box houses the master suite; on the top of the box, beneath the original roof, the designers installed a study.

The original rear block was demolished and replaced with a new three-story structure housing the kitchen on the ground floor and guest quarters above. By placing this block to the rear of the property, the designers made space for a full-width courtyard between the two structures. By putting a second staircase in the rear volume, the designers kept the connection between the two structures to a minimal steel and wood plane.

The designers installed a triple-height glass wall between the dining room at the rear of the sandstone box—the dining room is also three stories high—and the courtyard, supporting it with round timbers. In addition to establishing the inside/outside character of the dining room/courtyard volume, the glass walls allow light to penetrate deeply into the main volume. By tilting the sandstone clad wall of the rear building skywards, the designers made a reflector that also bounces light into the main building.

A view down into the dining room from the roof terrace of the new rear structure.

Seen from the roof of the rear building, the courtyard's blue-tiled pool with a curved edge makes a nice counterpoint to the rectilinearity of the structure. This view helps illuminate the depth of the building from eave to ground level.

A spa pool tiled in transparent blue glass serves as a focal point in the courtyard, enhancing the play of light in the interiors and shifting the emphasis to the connection between inside and outside, "preventing the shop house from feeling too internal," notes Hassell. A rooftop terrace on the new rear building allows the residents to gain further access to the outside.

Materials include Chinese granite flooring, teak timber work, and Indian sandstone. The original rough brick party walls, which step back in thickness as they rise, were left rough and painted to contrast with the smooth new elements. The new sandstone box has a steel frame, with columns containing all services. Considering the constricting narrowness of the original building, the designers have done a fine job of creating interiors that feel open, spacious, and light.

◇ A drawing of the dining room and the window wall between it and the courtyard, done prior to construction, lends a sense of the dramatic impact of this tall, glassed-in space.

◇ Early perspective across swimming pool, with new kitchen and guest quarters structure to left, main building to right, entry foyer at far right. The dining room lies just to the right of the courtyard, with the living room and master suite stacked to the right of the dining room and a study level tucked in under the existing eaves. In the final plan (see section) the designers added a fourth bathroom next to the study.

singapore residence

WOHA DESIGNS (WONG MUN SUMM AND RICHARD HASSELL)

Singapore

The front entrance presents an elegantly simple composition, a wooden door flanked by a potted plant.

First floor and second floor plans show how the house is designed as a trio of linked pavilions loosely wrapping around the pool. With tropical plantings all around, the pool's rectilinear form helps loosen the tightness of the angular site.

This home in Singapore was designed in response to a seemingly contradictory set of demands. The young professional couple that commissioned the project wanted an open house and security; tropical style cross-ventilation and air conditioning; outdoors-orientation and complete privacy; informality and urban style; finally, they yearned for links to the traditions of Asia, yet also wanted to be fresh and contemporary. In addition to these conflicting requirements, the designers were faced with a difficult, triangular-shaped quarter-acre lot, ringed with other houses, upon which the clients had already begun design of a house with another architect.

The team from WoHa started over, and developed a design that consisted of three linked pavilions surrounding a central swimming pool—a private, central space that all the rooms look into that is completely shielded from the outside. The public rooms are downstairs, the master suite and other bedrooms and bathrooms upstairs.

The architectural expression emerges in two themes: the pavilions are built of timber with tiled, pitched roofs, while the connecting structures are flat-roofed, with plain walls—counterpoint to the heavy timbers—that slide under the pitched roofs.

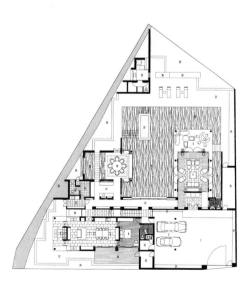

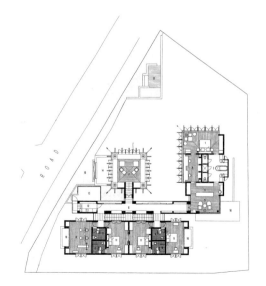

These views of the living and dining pavilions illustrate how the designers have seamlessly integrated the interior spaces around the swimming pool and adjacent reflecting pool area.

House and pool form a single, harmonious entity. By making the pool rectilinear in form, and then surrounding it with tropical landscaping, the designers overcame the compressed feeling of the site, instead creating a space that feels much larger than it is. Breezes and changing light on the pool affect the quality of light in the house; deep overhangs shield the interiors from monsoon rain and splashing water, yet allow the house to be left open during storms. Ceiling fans provide cross-ventilation, but a system of sliding, folding, and pocket doors allow the house to be completely closed up for air conditioning, and for security.

The interiors have been seamlessly integrated with the architecture, with many finishes flowing from the inside out. Ochre-colored, polished, and waxed cement forms the flooring, inside and out, connecting the varied finishes including gold Chinese granite, honey-colored Malaysian Balau timber, and charcoal Otta Phyllit stone. Built in, space-defining cabinets (some house air-conditioning units), made of teak, oak, cherry, and walnut, have been clad with mirrors to reflect the gardens, further dissolving the barriers between inside and outside. The same granite used in polished and honed form inside is used in rubble walls in the garden, and as rounded river pebbles to cover monsoon storm drains.

This perspective rendering was made by the architect prior to beginning the project, as part of the presentation to the client. A comparison with finish photographs shows that the drawing succeeded in conveying the projected relationship of inside and outside, and of the pool and the surrounding pavilions and gardens.

The family room exhibits a harmonious blend of Eastern and Western styles and forms. The task lamps were custom-designed for the house, utilizing abstracted versions of traditional Chinese and Malay forms.

The clients originally requested traditional, heavy timber furniture with soft fabrics and cushions, but the designers felt that approach was inappropriate for the light, indoor/outdoor style of the house. Instead, Wong Mun Summ developed a suite of custom pieces that incorporated the client's requirements, yet mixed the heavy timber with slatted open panels and padded Thai silk cushions to keep it cool and light. The designers integrated lighting into the design, choosing to highlight the "rhythms of the construction" with recessed uplights and downlights. Custom lamps in contemporary versions of Chinese and Malay forms were developed for task lighting.

With a client who was quite serious about cooking, the kitchen was a major element, and complicated by the need for two sections, in the Asian tradition: the open air "wet" kitchen is used for the more pungent Asian cooking, while the air conditioned "dry" kitchen is for Western cooking. In both areas, the design integrates custom stainless equipment with timber and mirror cabinets, and granite flooring.

Steeped in Asian tradition yet representing the best values of modern design, this residence offers a warm, dynamic and appealing fusion of East and West, brilliantly realized on a tight urban site.

The kitchen—actually there are two parts to it, a "wet" Asian kitchen that is more out-of-doors, and this part, the "dry" Western kitchen that is more enclosed and air conditioned. The coolness of stainless steel fixtures is warmed by the wooden floors and doors, and the generous amounts of daylight flowing in.

A detail of the dining room furniture. Seating, tables, and light fixtures were all custom-designed for the house.

An early sketch of the bathroom shows the ceiling forms, the privacy doors at left, and the sinks and tub at right, pretty much as they ended up being built.

View of the spacious, high-ceilinged master bathroom. The glass doors create privacy zones. Skylights enhance the richly daylit bathroom interior.

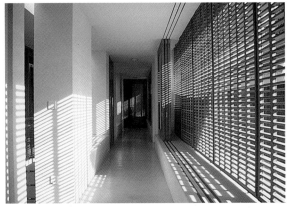

View of a gallery and the master bedroom show how window treatments screen the sun yet allow plenty of daylight into the house. The bedroom appears to be surrounded by a tropical rain forest, creating a completely private effect.

townhouse r

FAULDING ARCHITECTS
New York, New York

Dream about how you would like to live, from the "foundation to the bed sheets." That's the motto of Faulding Architects when the firm begins a new design project. Architect Heather Faulding and interior designer Margaret Davis encourage the client to begin with an open slate and slowly, layer upon layer, determine the specifics of a design program. In the case of Townhouse R, the result is a whimsical interior that highlights the client's unique interests and tastes.

First of all, the client needed to be encouraged to remain at this townhouse in New York City's Upper East Side. It helped that the architect promised to add 20 feet (6 meters) to the rear, as the townhouse was originally only 48 feet long (14.4-meters long) and 15 feet wide (4.65 meters wide). At the same time, this allowed the addition of bay windows in the rear, which would bring more natural light into the interiors.

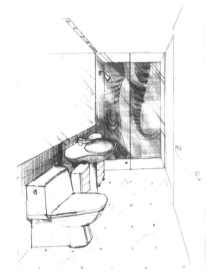

⊗ Rendering of the first floor bathroom.

⊗ The owner's intrigue with elephants is reflected in the glass mosaic mural on the shower wall in the nanny's bathroom.

⊗ Twenty feet (6 meters) were added to the rear of the four-story townhouse, which was originally only 48 feet (14.4 meters) long. Bay windows allow a great deal of natural daylight into the interiors.

⊗ Elevation of the townhouse.

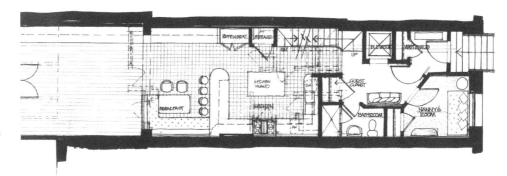

First floor plan includes the entry, kitchen, family room.

Lit by an overhead fluorescent light, the kitchen connects to the family room and features built-in custom cabinetry.

The basic plan completely stripped the interior surfaces. Then the fantasy started. As seen in the elevation, the townhouse proved large enough to adequately house the many activities required by the client, including a guest bedroom, a nanny's room, and even room on the second or main living area for a grand piano. What makes the interior unique is the attention to details and details are what means the most to the owners—the elephant mosaic in the first floor bathroom, the ocean theme in the children's bathroom, the gentler garden theme in the master bedroom.

Success must be attributed to the process undertaken by Faulding and Davis. Faulding calls it "reading the client's soul." She encourages exploratory research—through magazines, books, whatever sources are available, to find objects and scenes that elicit happiness and comfort. From there, the designing begins. Concepts are offered in two- and three-dimensional interpretations. These are used as a springboard for other ideas or incorporated into the final design. Most important is developing a "trusting relationship" with the client.

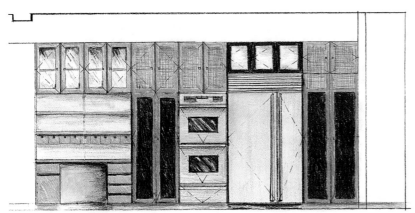

Elevation drawing of the kitchen cabinets.

The den features customized shelves.

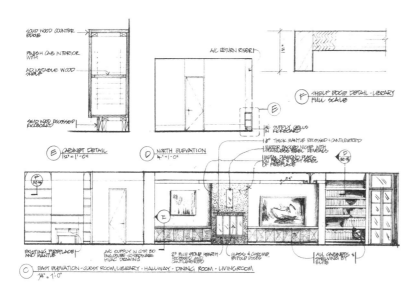

East elevation of the second floor, featuring the guest bedroom, library, hallway, dining room, and living room.

The owner of the house is a pianist, so a room for a full size grand piano was designed as part of the second floor living and dining room.

Sketch of the living room.

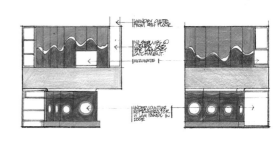

The laundry room reflects the nautical theme that occurs in the children's bathroom.

Elevation drawing of the laundry/kitchenette.

LAUNDRY/KITCHENETTE

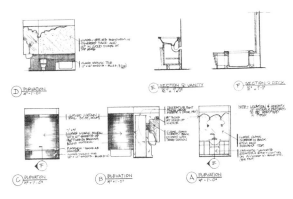

⊗ Renderings of the children's bathroom and details reveal the bathtub as a boat.
⊘

⊗ The children's bathroom features a glass mosaic mural of the ocean. The bathtub is the boat.

⊗ The designer's whimsy is seen in the hand-painted cabinetry in the children's room.

⊘ Even the bedcover in the master bedroom was custom designed.

⊘ The master bath is separated with glass doors so that it can be one larger room or three separate areas. The shower-bathtub area is also a steam room.

modern living space

CECCONI SIMONE, INC.

Toronto, Canada

The low-level dining room table and chairs maximize the look of a regular-height ceiling. Kitchen, dining and living rooms are combined into a 600-square-foot (54-square-meter) room.

In the new millennium we will seek sanctuary from the high-tech world in a natural "oasis" ready-made for the apartment dweller. That is the vision suggested by Cecconi Simone in its design for a Modern Living Space for the 1999 Interior Design Show in Toronto. Designers were asked to reflect upon contemporary living in a 600-square-foot (54-square meter) living space. Cecconi Simone based its design on the amalgamation of four basic elements—fire, earth, air, and water.

The modern nomadic culture needs a living space that is flexible, so concluded designers Anna Simone and Elaine Cecconi. At the same time, the apartment dweller needs a "sanctuary away from the chaotic everyday information overload, a place where one reposes and reflects." And, given rising real estate costs and shrinking living quarters, that place is likely to be composed of minimal square footage, particularly if located in a popular city. The designers were also environmentally conscious, as "direct interaction with natural surroundings and concern for the planet are integral to well-being

The chairs can be used at the table or pulled back as a banquette.

The designers see the apartment of the future as a quiet oasis, a sanctuary away from the high-tech world.

Floor plan shows how pieces fit together in minimal amount of space.

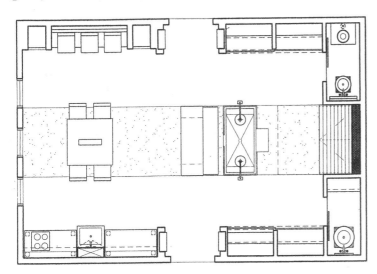

in the twenty-first century landscape," in the designer's words. Therefore, finishes that are usually reserved for outdoor use, such as sisal and concrete which are used inside to "bring the outside in" and to "challenge traditional notions of what makes a comfortable home." Gone are the usual accoutrements that adorn contemporary homes, such as PCs, microwave ovens, and oversized televisions. Found instead are "soothing features," such as an indoor herb garden, a candle-fired fireplace, and a roomy-two person shower.

The space is a progression of cooking, dining, and living spaces. Central to the space is a Japanese-style dining table, set low as to not dominate the room. Around it are custom-designed chairs, which can be pulled to the wall to serve as a sofa. A two-person shower occupies the area behind the translucent glass panels. The quiet zone is at the far end—a wood-seating area, over which a crimson-cushioned Murphy bed folds down at night. Backlit sail-cloth paneled doors that encase closets—critical storage space for a small apartment—as well as a small home office flank the recessed bed.

All of the furniture is built into the space, so essentially the occupant can move in with only his or her wardrobe and personal items. Once settled, the herb garden allows one to "indulge the senses by preparing and dressing foods with freshly grown greens." And the bathing area "brings emphasis to the understated luxury of the bath, both as a ritual and a place of retreat." The candles are then lit in the fireplace and the ambience is set.

⬡ Set behind translucent glass panels, the bath has an oversized tub and double-headed showerheads.

When the day bed is withdrawn, a comfortable platform is revealed.

The herb garden is built into the kitchen counter. Sisal and concrete are used throughout the design.

gaylord residence remodel

GGLO ARCHITECTS
Seattle, Washington

⌃ In this Seattle kitchen renovation the architect specified finishes in multiple tones to break up the runs of built-in cabinets. A terrazzo-topped island and a colorful, multi-hued splashback offer a pleasing balance of contemporary style and traditional warmth.

⌄ Rough plan of kitchen with new center island; drawing shows plan for the central island and the overhead glass fixture.

Three years after moving his family into an early 1960s colonial-style Seattle house, architect Bill Gaylord (a founding partner of the Seattle firm GGLO) elected to do a moderate remodel, centered around a major kitchen renovation, in an effort to make the house more livable. With its low ceilings and miniscule kitchen the house was dated—especially the kitchen. Notes Gaylord: "The kitchen is the center of every house, and I wanted to be able to eat and read newspapers and have plenty of room to invite twenty people over without it ever feeling too crowded."

Gaylord commissioned a local contractor to gut the kitchen and adjacent breakfast nook, then installed the new kitchen, with a more appealing plan achieved by pushing one wall out to expand the space. The new kitchen revolves around a central island: 4 by 11 feet (1.2 x 3.3 meters) in size, the cherry wood island features a countertop of terrazzo laced with green and umber recycled glass, iridescent mother of pearl, and café au lait-toned marble chips. The top is recessed at both ends, to lend it a more table-like appearance—specifically, it is meant to resemble a library table.

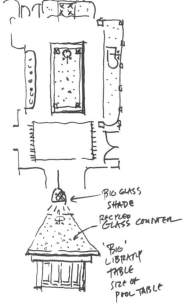

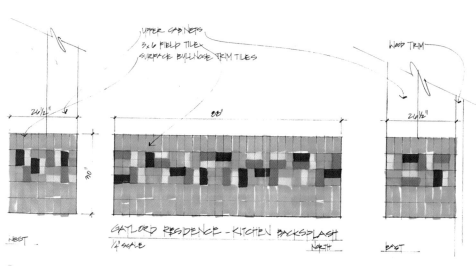

⌃ Color drawings show the architect's plan for the kitchen splashback, with its multi-hued tiles.

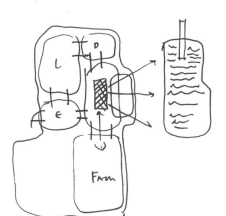

Rough sketches show the kitchen elevation with cabinets and a central table, and a plan addressing the relationship of interior to exterior.

View into the completed kitchen, drawn prior to construction.

With seven sets of French doors featuring beveled glass distributed throughout the house, Gaylord went with the same look for the eighteen-foot-long (5.4 meter-long), multipane window bay that now floods the kitchen with daylight, transforming it into a "conservatory." Artificial light from sunken ceiling and under-cabinet fixtures, and custom fixtures including a pair of striking pendant lamps over the terrazzo island, enrich the rich wash of daylight. To break up the runs of cabinets and make built-in pieces stand out more sharply, the architect specified a variety of finishes and colors—most in coffee tones, reflecting Gaylord's, and his wife's, love of coffee. A tile backsplash, also featuring multiple coffee tones, adds another dynamic color element to the space, enriching the fine balance of contemporary style and old-fashioned warmth.

Elsewhere in the house, though Gaylord was unable to raise the seven foot, ten inch ceilings, he at least made them look higher by increasing the scale of the trim, such as the crown moldings over the doors. Beyond this clever manipulation, Gaylord's primary tool for change and visual variety was color. The kitchen features coffee tones; the dining room, on the other hand, glows with a rich pumpkin shade, selected to highlight the reddish tansu, or Japanese chest, that stands in a corner of the room.

Early sketch of kitchen as library. The architect pushed out one wall to expand space and also to create a light-drenched, conservatory-like quality in the kitchen.

Gaylord is a collector, and his house was planned, in part, to display collections. Recessed shelves built into the walls between kitchen and dining room house a collection of over 600 salt-and-pepper shaker sets. A rotating wire postcard rack displays a collection of postcards in the family room, adding a whimsical touch to this pale blue room designed around a warming fireplace. In every room, artworks from contemporary Seattle artists mingle with pieces made by the architect's daughter.

The master suite was rearranged as well, with a wall removed primarily to simplify circulation from bedroom to bath. Three pairs of mirrored doors were added to increase light in the room, visually expanding the dressing room area. In the bathroom, Gaylord installed a pedestal sink for himself, and a traditional vanity for his wife, these unmatched pieces reflecting their different styles—styles that have been artfully integrated in every room of this warm family home.

⊘ Warm, pumpkin-toned walls set off the Japanese tansu chest in the dining room. The table is a classic Corbu, the chairs from a thrift shop.

⊘ Views of various exterior facades and elevations, and a living room layout, all drawn by the architect during the planning process.

Multiple pairs of French doors connect the living room with adjacent decks. Quirky contemporary artworks mix easily with casual, comfortable furnishings.

The master bath, with his and her unmatched sinks, hers in the vanity on this side of the wall, his the pedestal just visible on the other.

protti apartment

CARUZZO RANCATI RIVA ARCHITETTI ASSOCIATI

Milan, Italy

SCALE:

The Protti apartment lies within a large residential apartment complex erected near the Milan Fair in the 1960s; the densely-built area is punctuated with greenscapes, according to principal designer Letizia Caruzzo of Caruzzo Rancati Riva, the Milan firm which recently renovated the apartment's interiors. Caruzzo describes the area as possessing a "polished '60s-style architectural language." Her firm's design for the Protti apartment establishes what she describes as an "organic character for the layout as opposed to a rigid functional subdivision," suggesting an effort to reflect the area's mix of rectilinear built density alternating with the softer terrain of greenspace. Caruzzo is wordsmith as well as designer—at least in translation—and so perhaps her own words set the scene most tellingly: "We hope that our design approach reflects something of the unity of the details, tumult of the whole recommended by Abbe Laugier and reutilized by Le Corbusier as a synthetic definition of a compositional mode capable of combining the principles of rationality with the need for expressive impact." In other words, to balance the rationalism with voluptuousness, add some curves to the mix. It makes things a whole lot sexier.

◈ The floor plan shows how the centrally located spine wall serves as the focal object in the apartment, with the spaces arrayed around it, starting with the entry hall at top center. The slants and curves of various walls disrupt the rectilinear geometry of the space, creating a sense of movement through the apartment.

◇ In this early black-and-white drawing, the designers have already established the importance of the wall, far right, with its horizontal wood ribbing that lends a sense of movement through the space from the entry at far right rear into the living room in foreground. The idea of laying the wood floor on the diagonal, shown here, was realized in the final plan.

CASA PROTTI

Color drawing shows a view of the living and dining room area, with the wood paneled wall at rear. The counterpoint of curving, organic forms and rectilinear space planning, broken up by curves (not shown) in the wall, is replicated in the varying forms of the furnishings.

The dining table and lightweight chairs have a classic Modern look; the table's oval shape plays off the wall's curve at left.

This view of the living room shows the clean, elegant furnishings set against the richness of the walnut-clad wall element in the background. Pieces include a divan and a large elliptical hassock covered in wool with black leather borders, an armchair with headrest and footrest in yellow leather, and cylindrical tables finished in brushed sheet metal. Display niches hold a few select items at right.

The hallway leading to the dining room and living room is finished in horizontal walnut stave cladding. The orange/brown tone is a special finish called coccio pesto, nicely offsetting the wood and plaster.

The apartment originated with a traditional layout, which the new design "disrupts" in an effort to create a more fluid space—not a volume that reads as completely open and loft-like, but one that makes a sense of movement, of "circulation and osmosis among the various rooms...tangibly present," notes Caruzzo. The main element that creates this sense of movement is a wall, clad entirely in horizontal staves of Italian walnut, leading from the entrance to the living and dining areas. As is evident in the drawings made prior to the renovation, and in the resulting plan and photographs, the designers envisioned and developed this wall as a focal "object" in the apartment, with various rooms organized around it, and large storage closets built into it and accessible from both sides. The wall terminates in a semi-circular curve that signals passage to the apartment's office. The angled and curving wall, described by Caruzzo as an "organic volumetric divider," heightens the sense of perspective and thus visually enlarges the space. Along with various oval-shaped and circular pieces of furniture, the wall form also provides shapely contrast to the rectilinear perimeter walls and windows.

A sliding door in the wall leads to the master bedroom suite, where the orthogonal plan, as expressed by the straight line of the closet (the "back" of the walnut-clad wall) is countered by another curving wall that encloses the bathroom. These two elements—one curving, one straight—converge in a passage that Caruzzo describes as a "perspective funnel" that leads to the apartment's office and an adjacent terrace.

On a more traditional note, the designers situated the guestroom and bath to one side of the entry; on the other, beyond a sliding door, they placed the kitchen, maid's bed and bathroom, and service areas.

Caruzzo specified a palette of materials that contributes to the synthesis of opposing formal elements. The central spine wall is clad in Italian walnut, its horizontal ribbing creating a sense of flow through the space. The teakwood floor has been laid on the diagonal throughout, helping pull the various volumes together, then decorated with a few well-chosen, warmly colorful Asian throw rugs. The designers finished the walls in a light Mantuan stucco, then added a natural orange shade called "coccio pesto" on columns in the living room to create a warm contrast with the natural wood. The master bath features an ice-toned gravel composite flooring, countered by glass mosaic walls. The guest bath balances gray gravel with opaline facings, while the kitchen floor has been finished in brick tones to reflect the natural copper color of the metal panels. Throughout the apartment, carefully selected pieces of classic modern and contemporary furniture have been artfully integrated with works ranging from striking modern paintings to fragments of tiles and buildings from the Renaissance and Gothic periods. The whole effect is one of elegant harmony, unmistakably up to date in tone, yet graced with a deep richness of form and material that lends these interiors a timeless quality.

⊘ A view of the master bedroom, with the bed flanked by an elliptical table in black leather and another table made of walnut. The painting is called "Landscape of the Heart," by Claude Caponnetto, from 1990. The walnut-clad wall unit, forming a straight line on this bedroom side, is visible at left.

⊘ The master bathroom features a curving shower stall and cabinets made of burnished metal and panes of translucent glass, counterpointed with a chrome-plated metal mirror.

⊘ The walnut ribbing extends down the wall in the bedroom side, where the wall becomes a closet, with rather exotic iguana door handles. The pieces on the shelves are archaeological fragments from Gothic and Renaissance ruins.

◇ A view of the circular shower with an adjacent cabinet abstracts the forms, celebrating the simple richness of burnished metal and translucent glass.

◇ A long view of the primary wall suggests how it interacts with the apartment's essentially rectilinear geometry, transforming it into a less predictable, more fluid kind of space.

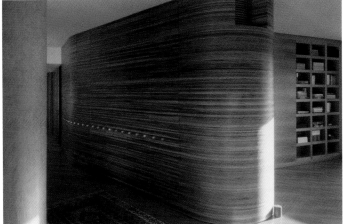

◈ This passage between wooden walls leads from the master bath back toward the apartment office. The convergence of the walls creates a forced "perspective funnel" effect.

◇ An intersection of various forms and materials in a hallway demonstrates the dynamic interaction that infuses the apartment with energy and motion—and warmth, from the mix of woods and other soft, organic tones and shapes.

◈ View from the head of the bed in the master bedroom shows the "perspective funnel" created by the convergence of the straight line of the closet structure at right and the curving wall that encloses the bathroom at left.

ghaiss apartment

CARUZZO RANCATI RIVA ARCHITETTI ASSOCIATI

Beirut, Lebanon

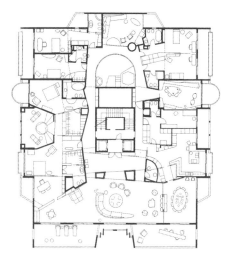

⊙ Continuous floor plan (without key) shows rooms wrapping around central core and circulation corridor, with living room at bottom (with two matched terraces) flanked by the dining room on the right and the office at far left below the master suite. The master suite includes his and hers bed, bath, and dressing rooms, with the two wings separated by the whirlpool tub at left center. The children's rooms occupy the upper section, wrapped around the children's gym enclosed in the semi-circle at the top of the core. The right side includes a family room, staff quarters, and the kitchen that adjoins the dining room.

Once celebrated as the most beautiful and cosmopolitan city on the Mediterranean, Beirut is in the process of emerging from decades of strife, for it has been one of the flash points in the seemingly endless Arab-Israeli conflict. At present parts of the city still have something of a bombed-out look, with mountains of rubble and broken-down streets and buildings alternating with new and rebuilt construction. Along the city's coastline, a number of new and old residential apartment towers, some of then containing rambling, multi-room apartments, have been occupied continuously or recently built and/or reoccupied. Architect Letizia Caruzzo of the Milan design firm Caruzzo Rancati Riva (CRR) describes the scene as "a heaped together insertion along the coast, of residential towers characterized by a configuration as versatile as it is disenchanted and chaotic." The vacation apartment shown on these pages, designed for the Ghaiss family by CRR, occupies a floor in one such tower. "Versatile" here implies that anything goes, notes Caruzzo: "...ample freedom was left to the desires of the client and the intentions of the architect; in fact, except for the core of stairs and other structural constraints, it was possible to work with great flexibility in defining the distribution of the plan and its formal character."

Caruzzo describes the vast, luxurious apartment as "a villa suspended, inclined towards the landscape but turned in toward its interior." The intention, she notes, was "to give voice to the client's expressive exuberance" via "an expressionist configuration" based on "accentuations and deformations of volumes and spaces, and on the dialogue among diverse and at times precious materials, capable of generating unusual and dissonant harmonies." For all its oblique, slightly overwrought intellectualism, Caruzzo's language does, in fact, capture something of the rich eclecticism of the apartment, which mingles the sleek and the chic, neo-traditionalism and ultramodernism, with easy aplomb.

In the entry, the steel walls are burnished to flicker and flare with plays of shadow and light. The black granite floor that begins here extends into the living and dining rooms. The yellow portal echoes the traditional color of front doors in Beirut.

The living room as seen in an early drawing. The wall separating living from dining room has already been designed, with its four vertical, curving cabinets. The yellow wall at left has openings into the entry. The furnishings turned out a little differently, but the essential look, including the black granite floor, is already in place.

Considering the unusually eclectic approach taken here, preliminary "prepping" of the clients was of great importance. By working up a set of drawings, prior to construction, which showed in some detail the way the apartment would look, the architect was able to give the client a real sense of what to expect. Though the drawings and the finished product are not exact matches, they're close enough to make it clear the client knew what it were getting, and happily, it got it.

The apartment essentially follows a continuous plan, generated by the centrally located elevator and stairs. Adjacent to this arrival core the designers installed a spacious entry vestibule, finished in burnished steel and entered via a heavy yellow door (yellow is the traditional color of front doors in Beirut), with a rough finish that contrasts with the smoother steel of the vestibule. As is evident in the floor plan, the entry vestibule extends to form a circulation corridor that completely encircles the arrival core, with the apartment then encircling the vestibule. This circulation corridor changes shape along the way, with angles and curves adding visual interest, and also helping to create the "accentuations and deformations of volumes and spaces" sought by the architect. It also shifts from a black granite floor in the vestibule and the more "public" rooms to a wood floor in the private areas.

From the vestibule the primary openings lead to the living room, the apartment's largest space. Here, a segmented wall that contains and shapes the room is counterpointed by a window wall (opening onto a pair of decks) on the opposite side. At one end, a translucent sandblasted glass wall, anchored with a row of four curving, wooden storage units, separates the living room from the dining room. At the other end, the living room narrows, forcing the perspective; the slanting wall, finished in walnut, encloses a small study.

The study adjoins the master suite, with two sleeping areas, one predominantly finished in white leather and the other in walnut. A large, marbled whirlpool bathing and relaxing area separates them, with nearby water closet/bath facilities luxuriously finished with marble. The remainder of the apartment consists of a series of rooms including studies, children's bedrooms, playrooms, and bathrooms, all of which are accessed by the interior circulation corridor. The children's bedrooms are designed with each individual child in mind: the older daughter's room features a soft palette of pale lacquers and hand-finished walls; the first-born son's has an ebony finish, while the youngest child's room is finished in intense blues, with nautical theming. The children also have their own movie viewing room, and in the core, enclosed by a curving glass wall, a small gymnasium with a sauna and a whirlpool tub.

Between the children's zone and the kitchen, a family room has been designed with a sofa specifically created to evoke the looks of a luxury car from the 1950s. The kitchen, with staff quarters on one side and dining room on the other, features a palette of white lacquer and stainless steel, with curving surfaces to soften the hardness of the materials; the most dramatic curve forms the corridor connecting the kitchen with the dining room.

The furnishings palette—indeed the look and style of the residence—has been established primarily for the family's comfort; but also, notes Caruzzo, to engender "recouping of the autochthonous history and culture through the insertion of rare fragments, furniture, and traditional quilted objects, creating a narration all aimed at a high level of agitation, supported by a powerful visual language—from German Expressionism to Russian Constructivism and of the modern avant garde in general." And several balconies providing great views of the Mediterranean. Hopefully this essay in tastefully extravagant design will survive whatever wars the region throws at it.

Color drawing shows an early version of the eldest daughter's bedroom. The form at far right evolved into a rich, dark wooden bookcase and storage unit, while the furnishings in the room are more spare and simple than those drawn here. But the spirit is essentially there already in the drawing.

In the private areas the centrally located circulation path has a wooden floor, seen here by the translucent curves of the glass-paneled wall that encloses the kids' gymnasium.

Color drawing shows the gymnasium located at one end of the core. The circulation path winds around it, separating the perimeter rooms from the central core. The curving red form at left is part of a cylindrical form that curves into the movie room on the other side. The glass panels enclosing the gym are sandblasted in the apartment as built, rendering the interior more private.

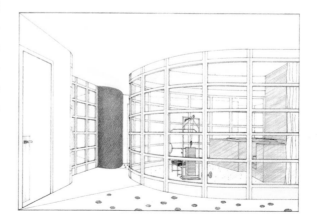

⊗ The kitchen gleams with stainless steel and white lacquer finishes against the black floor; the hard surfaces are softened by sleek, curving edges.

⊘ The "her" section of the master suite, imagined in advance. Again, many specific elements from this drawing were changed or eliminated in the built space, but the essence remains the same—an eclectic balance of traditional opulence and modern simplicity.

⊘ The movie room, as seen in an early drawing; the architectural elements and major finishes and fixtures are already set, though specifics changed as the apartment was built.

⊘ Drawing of the office in the master suite, with modern furnishings and rich, warm wood walls and finishes.

tribeca loft

L.A. MORGAN

New York City

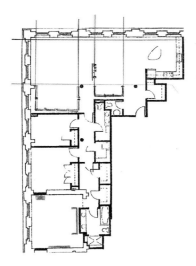

Floor plan shows main room at top, with lighter lines indicating the locations of the two glass screens the designer created to even the room up. The fifty-one-foot-long (15.3-meter-long) volume includes an open kitchen at top right, dining area at top center, and living room area at top left. The three rooms below are bedrooms and an office.

This version includes sketched in furnishings, including the three towers placed within the enclosure of the large U-shaped glass screen at the bottom of the living area, upper left.

Loft living at its best should balance the openness of the old factory volumes with the more private, intimate spaces associated with life at home. L.A. Morgan's design for this loft has achieved this balance, giving his clients the best of both worlds.

Created for a young family with two small children and an energetic dog, this New York loft story begins, like most authentic loft stories, with an old factory in downtown Manhattan, in the *tres chic* neighborhood of Tribeca. (For those who don't know, Tribeca is short for Triangle Below Canal, and it refers to a neighborhood tucked in between SoHo to the north, Chinatown to the east, and Wall Street to the south). The conversion to residential space is fairly recent, meaning that this new home represents the first post-industrial use of the 3,000-plus-square-foot (270-plus-square meter) loft. In planning the residence Morgan set out to create "a serene, restful space that is user-friendly and adaptable as well as stylish."

His conversion of the space was completed without structural alterations to the existing floor plan. Instead, all the surfaces were refinished: wooden floors sanded and stained a dark ebony brown, walls painted pale gray-white. According to Morgan, "the design is installed within the existing shell of the apartment, creating a new layer of design set apart from the walls created by the developer."

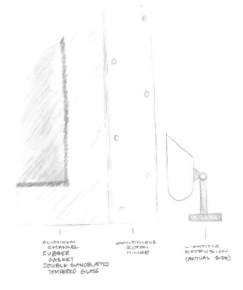

Drawing shows a corner detail of a glass screen, with component materials identified. The roton hinge offers strength, flexibility, and a very clean looking finish; at right, a drawing of the custom uplight designed for the project.

Drawings show how the three oak storage/shelving towers float within the embrace of the deeper U-shaped glass screen adjacent to the seating area in the living room. The corner detail at right shows how the custom light fixture shown at bottom tucks in between the existing wall and the glass screen, providing backlight for the screen.

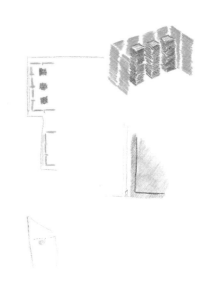

Two views of the "living room," a seating area in the sunlit southwest corner of the residence. Walls and floors were refinished; window treatments include solar scrims and linen roller shades. An Asante stool from Africa adds an exotic touch to the modern furniture palette. The painting at left, by David Row, is displayed on a custom-designed metal easel rather than hung on the wall.

A view of the three oak towers the designer created and sited within the enclosure formed by a deep, U-shaped glass screen. The sculpted towers contain books, electronic gear, and assorted objects but present a blank front to the room, minimizing visual clutter.

Those drawn to loft living generally like wide-open spaces; New York's original living lofts often had no doors or walls except those that enclosed the bathrooms. As the genre has developed and grown more sophisticated, clients have come to prefer designs that integrate a mix of open and enclosed spaces, and this project takes that approach. The main room, 51-feet (15.3-meters) long, faces south and west, with nine 8-foot-high (2.4-meter-high) windows. To balance the irregular widths of the room, Morgan installed a pair of custom-designed, backlit, U-shaped glass screens. Floating in front of and contrasting with the pale walls, these screens help define locations for the entrance hall, dining area, and the passage to the bedrooms and library area. As organized by the screens and existing walls, the generously scaled main volume has space enough for an open kitchen, the dining area, and a "living room" or seating area. In these open volumes and throughout, the designer has specified clean, modern furnishings or antiques that share the modern virtues of clarity and simplicity. For example, between the arms of the shallower of the two glass screens, the designer positioned an eighteenth-century Chinese scholar's cabinet, made of elm, which serves as both display stand and serving piece. One hears eighteenth-century Chinese antique and imagines something fussy, but this subtly wrought piece exhibits a clear, functional design.

The area shaped by the deeper glass screen houses three oak towers created by the designer for storage and display. With blind fronts facing into the living room, the three towers contain cubes for objects and books accessible from the sides only. The central tower houses the stereo system and a television, facing into the room but hidden, when not in use, behind a wooden panel. These three towers serve their utilitarian purposes, but also take on the aura and power of massive, minimalist sculpture: the designer refers to them as "Easter Island" objects.

The space features several unique light sources, all created, like the rest of the furnishings and fixtures and indeed, the entire space, to minimize the possibilities for damage to or by dogs and/or children. Mounted atop a pair of large black speakers, custom birdseye maple veneer lighting cubes provide a rich source of ambient light. Chrome reading lamps and a custom veneer lighting fixture floating over the dining table enhance the quality of light and add intriguing sculptural elements to the room. Daylight pours in from the oversized south and west exposure windows, modulated by solar veil scrims, with linen roller shades utilized for privacy.

The residents have collected paintings by noted contemporary artists including Robert Mangold and Sean Scully; the designer created custom steel easels to mount them, enhancing the sense of layering within the shell and keeping the walls free of clutter. In the office, an original Frank Gehry Easy Edges Cardboard Table serves as a work desk.

In the bedroom, the designer painted over the original brick walls with multiple layers of high gloss paint to eliminate all holes and marks. Two layers of window treatment—solar veil scrims with matching wood blinds—lend a sense of depth to the windows, while a pair of arched recesses that once held doors now contain a full length mirror framed in fabric and a built-in cantilevered desk made of birch. A birch screen, its U-shape echoing the glass screens in the living room, encloses the bed and a pair of nineteenth-century Chinese stands used as night tables, creating a warm, protected area within the coolness of the painted brick room.

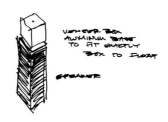

⊘ Drawings show custom-designed maple veneer light cubes resting atop massive black speakers, transforming them into simple light fixtures.

⊘ Views of the dining area positioned between open kitchen and living room area. Simple, sturdy furnishings make sense in a house with a small child and a large dog. Accessories on the tabletop include a Zulu staff and an antique bowling ball.

⊘ A Chinese scholar's cabinet from the nineteenth century glows serenely in the backlit enclosure of a U-shaped glass screen adjacent to the dining area. The piece can be used as a serving stand; in this image it displays a Koto wood veneer lamp by Ted Abramczyk, a pair of eighteenth-century Chinese bowl stands, and an African drum.

The bedroom includes a U-shaped birch screen, its form like the glass ones in the main room of the residence, that encloses the bed in a warm, inviting container within the cool, painted brick room. The nightstands are of nineteenth-century Chinese vintage. A birch shelf canted off the wall provides a surface for changing accessory display. The painting is by Erin Parish.

grinstein residence bathroom remodel

GGLO ARCHITECTS

Seattle, Washington

GRINSTEIN RESIDENCE   MASTER BATH - WEST   MASTER BATH - NORTH
1/2" = 1'-0"
GGLO ARCHITECTURE AND INTERIOR DESIGN
1/6/98

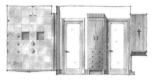

GRINSTEIN RESIDENCE   MASTER BATH - EAST   MASTER BATH - SOUTH
1/2" = 1'-0"
GGLO ARCHITECTURE AND INTERIOR DESIGN
1/6/98

MASTER BATH - NORTH

Drawn prior to construction, watercolor elevations of the bathroom's four walls, complete with fixtures, furnishings, and finishes, were used to give the client a sense of what the room would look like on completion. The final product bears a strong similarity to the drawings.

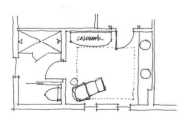
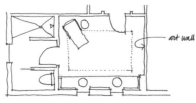

EARLY PLAN STUDIES

Though small in scale, this remodel of a 200-square-foot (18-square-meter) master bathroom in a private home in Seattle offers some appealingly expansive design ideas that transform an uninviting space into a welcoming spa. The in-city home belongs to the president and CEO of a communications company. Though the house is a light-filled contemporary gem on the shore of Lake Washington, the original master bath consisted of a series of small spaces connected by a narrow, dark corridor, that "severely compromised its functionality," notes Carol Deal Schaefer, principal in charge from GGLO.

The designers came up with a new concept for the bath, transforming the warren of small dark rooms into one large, comfortable volume, inspired by ancient spa baths, then scaling this space down into two zones divided by translucent, cast-glass panels. These panels provide a degree of privacy while maintaining a sense of open space. The two "zones" in the space consist of the wet zone and the dry zone. The dry zone, occupying approximately two-thirds of the space, includes sinks, vanities, and cabinets; the smaller wet zone contains the shower and water closet.

⊗ The architect added a winding exterior stair linking the bath-
⊘ room with a new rooftop deck. The contemporary house features a view east across Lake Washington from Seattle.

⊖ Prior to doing watercolor elevations, the designers drew
concept elevations of the four walls.

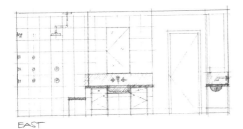

EAST

CONCEPT ELEVATIONS

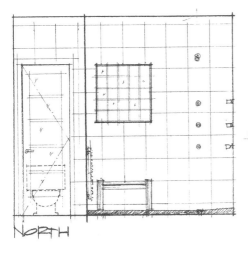

NORTH

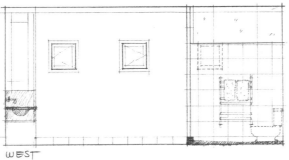

WEST

CONCEPT ELEVATIONS

The remodel of a 200-square-foot (18-square-meter) bathroom opened a cluster of small dark spaces into one large room, then divided it into two zones—"wet" and "dry". The larger "dry" zone includes the main vanity and flanking cabinets, all custom designed and constructed of cherry wood. The countertops and floors are slate, with radiant under-floor heat. Custom fixtures enhance the light from the square skylight carved into the ceiling at top. The sink in this vanity is stainless steel.

The basin on the south wall, also in the dry zone, is made of cast glass resting atop a slate-topped, steel-legged table —a minimalist counterpoint to the richer materials and forms on the east wall. Glass walls at right separate wet from dry zones while allowing visibility and an enhanced sense of spaciousness.

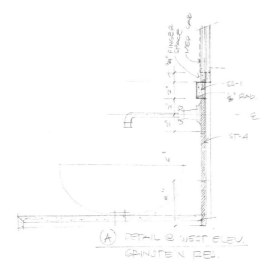

Detail drawing of the cast-glass basin and plumbing on the west wall.

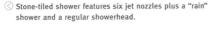

Stone-tiled shower features six jet nozzles plus a "rain" shower and a regular showerhead.

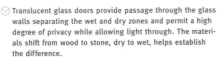

Translucent glass doors provide passage through the glass walls separating the wet and dry zones and permit a high degree of privacy while allowing light through. The materials shift from wood to stone, dry to wet, helps establish the difference.

The designers selected natural, nonsynthetic materials wherever possible, to evoke the feel of an ancient bath. Illumination comes from skylights, enhanced with stainless steel and glass sconces flanking the medicine cabinet. The custom-designed, full-height cabinets and matching vanity are made of cherry wood. Water sources emerge directly from stone tile walls; the basins are made of stainless steel or cast glass to match the glass partitions. Slate countertops and a radiantly heated slate floor add another natural element to the palette. To finalize the link with nature, a new circular stair links the bath with a rooftop deck offering spectacular views across Lake Washington.

In the wet zone the emphasis went not only to privacy but also to luxury in personal care; in addition to the heated slate floor and heated towel racks, the shower itself includes six body jets, a "rain" shower, and the main shower. Luxurious yet efficiently functional, the room offers what designer Schaefer terms "the symbiosis of spa-like luxury with practical daily use."

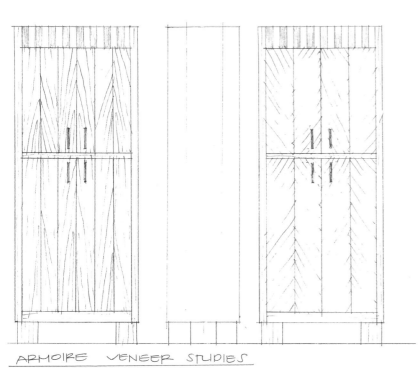

ARMOIRE VENEER STUDIES

Drawings of the custom armoire display different veneer options.

randy brown studio and residence

RANDY BROWN ARCHITECTS

Omaha, Nebraska

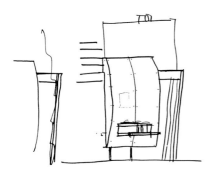

⊘ Early versions of the curved, metal-clad container wall with other components arranged to create an entry area.

⊘ The curving, metal-clad laminate wall partially encloses the dining/conference room; the table penetrates the wall, adding to the expressive quality of the space. The office studio lies to the left, separated from the conference room by a curving wall of shelving.

Located on one of Omaha's busiest boulevards, in a circa-1970s building that originated as a child care center, Randy Brown's new home and office offered the architect an opportunity to explore and demonstrate in a single, ongoing project various aspects of his working philosophy. Essentially, the 40 by 40 foot (12 meters by 12 meters) studio residence serves as a lab and work-shop, where Brown and his staff can demonstrate design and construction techniques as well as celebrate the benefits of green architecture. Making the new office in an existing structure underscores the firm's commitment to recycling—a commitment most strongly affirmed by re-use of the building itself, and furthered by the canny specification of salvaged materials ranging from lumber and light fixtures to nuts, bolts, and brackets. By putting his residence in the same interior that contains his office/studio, Brown allows prospective clients a first hand look at the pleasures and problems associated with living and working in one place. The arrangement of the various elements in the open, double-height volume offers these same clients a potent jolt of Brown's challenging architectural approach, which he expresses as "sculpting space to achieve continuity." They chose not to separate the rooms, "so the volume is one large, open, and dynamic interior." With the framing, ductwork, and piping left exposed, the structure also serves as an educational tool, where clients can see the "hidden" parts of a building design.

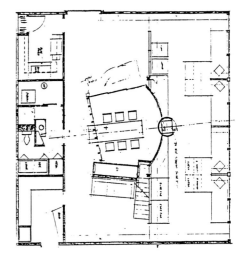

⊘
⊘ Drawings illustrate the development of the central, free-standing structure of bookcases, cabinets, and timber braces that enclose the dining/conference room and support the sleeping loft.

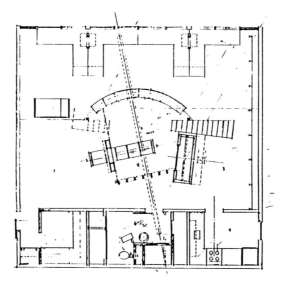

⊘ The curved wall of shelving at left separates the design studio from the dining/conference room. Bathed in natural light from south facing windows, the studio is furnished with desks designed and built on-site.

⊘ Exploded drawing shows the "kit of parts" that makes up the central container and the sleeping loft. Brown explains that the project was developed in a linear fashion, so that each part influenced the shape and size of the next.

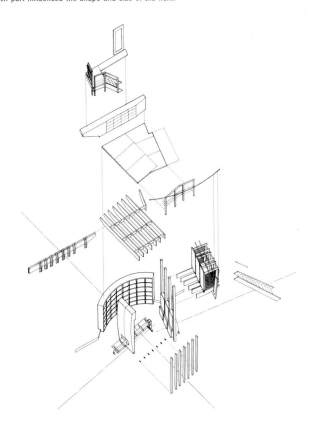

Randy Brown Architect's is an eight-person operation that includes Brown (he has degrees in both interior design and architecture), his wife, and a staff of six architects and interior designers. According to Brown, two or three staff members collaborate on every project. In design development they employ the usual tools: drawing board, computer, raw materials, three dimensional models—but Brown's methods are his own, for he is a hands-on design-builder, constantly experimenting with new and recycled materials and construction technology. The bandsaw in the office is not just for show.

On this project, Brown and his wife shared the lead roles, for obvious reasons: they had the most to gain or lose from the design, for they live and work there, and were creating not only a home for themselves and an office for the firm but also a promotional tool for their business. In doing the project, the Browns ignored two valuable pieces of advice most architects give their clients: don't live in a remodel while the work is being done, and don't do it yourself. Instead, they moved in, camped out, and started designing and building. Wisely, they began with the shower.

⊗ Two models of the building, one with a wall peeled away, reveal how the interior "container"
⊘ fits into the existing box.

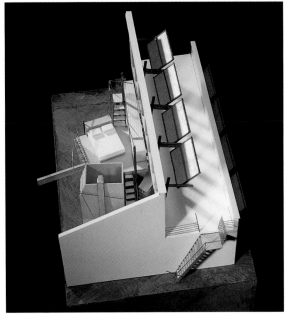

Timber braces and wood walls help define the central container, a dynamic structure with an open "ceiling" above that serves as floor for the sleeping loft. Note the shelves built into the inside of the metal-clad wall at the opposite end of the dining/conference table.

View of the stairs to the sleeping loft. The closet above offers a counterpoint to the wooden wall, below, that helps contain the conference/dining room.

Floor plan shows position of central container in the 40 by 40 foot (12 meters by 12 meters) box, with work areas, kitchen, bath, and storage along the peripheries.

The project gave Brown a chance to explore what he calls "design as a linear process." After putting in the shower, they built desks, and then bookcases to create separation. The kitchen followed, and then the platform for the sleeping loft. "We had the whole plan in our heads," he says, "but as each element was created," he says, "its scale and form influenced the design of the next. Usually we design holistically, but not here. We worked at full scale, using our own hands and tools. It was an incredible educational process."

The renovation began with a thorough stripping down of the existing structure, a 1970s passive solar box set well back—175 feet (53.5 meters)—from a busy street, with large windows facing south and a single pitch shed roof. Though in need of major repair, the building offered the virtue of a straightforward open floor plan, a generous interior volume that could serve as a stage for design experimentation, and a good-sized lot for additions and landscaping. Brown refinished the exterior with eye-catching white stucco and new low E glazing; inside, white paint on bare walls brightens the space and contrasts with the architectural objects and furniture. A splayed canopy now marks the entry, only hinting at the graceful radicalism of the interior architecture.

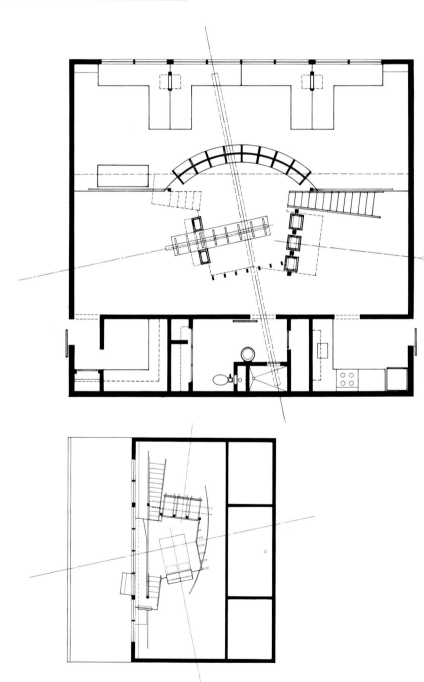

Plan of upper level sleeping loft.

The functional live/work interior components, including bath, kitchen, workstations, and storage space, surround the interior's central volume, which is not so much a "volume" as an oversized, surprisingly elegant object fairly bristling with distinct formal elements. This large piece of furniture—Brown calls it a "container"— is a freestanding structure composed of bookcases, cabinets, and angled timber braces that partially enclose the dining/conference room and support the sleeping loft overhead. With Brown seeing no need for separation between living and working areas, this central piece, which can be taken apart, moved, or expanded with a screwdriver and a couple of wrenches, becomes the project's primary focus, a multi-layered architectural stage for exploring different means of sculpting space and form to integrate the mixed functions of working andliving. These explorations are exemplified by the conference/dining table, an intriguing assemblage of raw wood, glass, metal extrusions, and casters; at one end, the plane of the table penetrates and connects to a curving metal-clad laminate sheet that simultaneously encloses the meeting/eating area, helps support the sleeping loft, and serves as a focal point for the entry area. The curved metal-clad wall doesn't touch the ground, the better to "push and pull space" says Brown, referring to the way his sculpted, strangely compelling yet functional forms animate the interior.

Though photographs, models, and drawings capture moments that lend a sense of permanence, Brown's home and office remain perpetually, delightfully unfinished, offering a never-ending exploration of the process of design.

⊘ Sleeping loft is linked to clerestory and roof catwalk by this short stair.

⊘ Table leg details

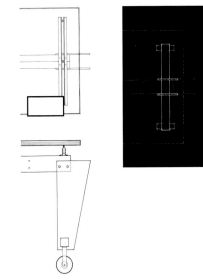

the cecil williams glide community house

MICHAEL WILLIS ARCHITECTS

San Francisco, California

⊗ By putting bay windows in the individual apartments, the designers increase the openings' apparent size and allow more light to penetrate.

"How do you convey comfort, optimism, and self-reliance to the dispossessed, while meeting a tight budget?" In the course of designing fifty-two units of transitional housing on a 6,000-square-foot (540-square-meters), dense urban site, Michael Willis Architects met the challenge implied by the question. The client, an inner-city congregation, owned the site adjacent to their church. In addition to the fifty-two units—studios as well as one-, two-, and three-bedroom apartments—the structure had to house administrative and social service offices, infant care areas, and indoor and outdoor gathering spaces. The budget was $10 million.

The design team responded with a nine-story building containing 50,627 square feet (4,703.5 square meters) of space. The midrise height complements the urban locale; the facade matches the scale of the neighboring buildings, while vertical bay windows echo the older buildings nearby.

⊗ The materials are low cost and the design is simple and spare, but the apartments are comfortable and spacious.

⊗ The ground floor infant day care center lies just off the courtyard.

⊘ Etched glass windscreens protect the rooftop deck from winds. The deck offers bright, sunny space for residents.
▸

A glass and limestone lobby conveys a welcoming air to visitors and residents alike. Recognizing the importance of creating comfortable social spaces so that residents could experience a sense of community and reintegration into society, the designers established a number of informal and organized gathering places. On the ground floor, in addition to the lobby they created an outdoor court, a multipurpose room with its own kitchen, and an infant care center. On the roof, a protected deck offers sweeping views. The basement contains intake rooms, conference rooms, and social service offices. The studios and apartments have been designed with generously scaled bay windows to maximize daylight and expand the sense of space.

⊗ Created in collaboration with a local artist, the limestone fountain in the ground floor courtyard is engraved with the lyrics to the congregation's favorite hymn, "Coming Home."

With little budget for decorative details, the designers found local artists to collaborate on pieces installed in public areas, such as the etched glass windscreens on the rooftop deck, and a limestone fountain in the lower courtyard that has been etched with the congregation's favorite hymn. The most dramatic element is uppermost: a swooping copper cornice hovers over the rooftop deck, its form drawn from traditional African headrests and stools. The striking piece elevates the project into a higher realm, reinforcing the sense of the building as a spiritual place, a place, notes the architect, "where all people are unconditionally accepted, and healing takes place."

◇ Drawings from early in the design process show various versions of roughly curving lines to suggest the shape of the rooftop form, and also place the building in its context between the church and an adjacent midrise building.

⊗ Exterior view of the building's façade show how it relates to the neighboring buildings in terms of scale and with vertical window openings. The swooping copper rooftop form, inspired by African headdresses and stools, points towards the adjacent church.

w hotel new york

ROCKWELL GROUP WITH HELPERN ARCHITECTS

New York, New York

⊗ Sample boards for the W Hotel palette show materials, colors, and textures based on the four elements: shown here, earth, water and fire.

The Rockwell Group worked design magic on a tired old dowager of a Manhattan hostelry to make the W Hotel, an urban oasis that owes a major debt of inspiration to of all things, in the up-tempo environs of 50th Street and Lexington Avenue, the natural world. At the W, the designers discovered the iconography of wellness in nature: "The elements of life—wind, water, earth, and fire—define the actual images, materials, color, and textures used throughout the building," notes David Rockwell. From this concept, rooted in the notion of these classically defined elements, a complex palette evolved, a narrative basis for four sets of materials and colors, distinct but related by virtue of their foundation in the natural world.

The Rockwell design team, led by senior associate-in-charge Edmund Bakas and director of interiors Alice Yiu, set out to transform the 1928 building into "a new concept in hospitality design—a wellness center in the heart of the city." Now that sounds intriguing, if a bit organic, for millennial Manhattan. And yet, along with organic, the W is nothing if not cool, hip, *au courant*—a trendy place in a trend-chasing city with upscale hotels lining every block. The Rockwell Group's talent for taking a motif or concept that could easily be rendered superficially, or overwhelmed by cliché, and instead making a grounded, meaningful, and yet *tres chic* design, continues to impress. How? By following through: whatever the motif or conceptual basis for a design, Rockwell designers explore it seriously, as deeply as time and money will permit. That willingness to explore tends to result in design that resonates with value, with meaning.

⊘ Color drawing of the lobby lounge illustrated the concept for the space in advance of construction, with mosaic tile window walls, high ceilings, and a light-toned palette creating an airy, spacious ambience.

⊗ Drawings of the renovated midtown Manhattan building, originally constructed in 1928, with new floors added on the roof and a striking, upwardly-angled glass canopy over the sidewalk at street level.

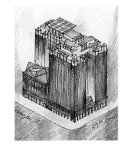

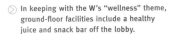
The W Hotel's new steel and sandblasted glass canopy lends the property a strong street presence in a neighborhood saturated with hotels.

Tiled columns and glass mosaic walls add color and excitement to the hotel's public spaces.

In keeping with the W's "wellness" theme, ground-floor facilities include a healthy juice and snack bar off the lobby.

This view of the lobby shows the comfortable, naturally-finished seating, "stump" gaming tables, fabric curtains at left, and glass mosaic walls with embedded leaves at far right. Double-height ceilings lend the room a sense of grandeur, light, and spaciousness.

Prior to finishing the interiors with this evocative palette, the design team engaged in a major architectural renovation of the existing structure, seeking to reorganize and expand public spaces and guestroom counts while dramatizing the hotel's street presence. The designers began by stripping away a bricked-in front section on the second floor, opening up space for a lounge that rises to double height; the move also exposed arched windows overlooking the street. Two more floors were added on the roof, raising the room count to 725 (including 50 suites). On the street level, a new canopy constructed of seven transparent, tempered glass panels supported on beams and columns of brushed stainless steel juts out over the sidewalk to offer shelter for taxi-seekers. It also provides the property with an eye-catching visual note at the entry, distinguishing the W from the other hotels on the block.

Public spaces occupying the lower levels subtly evoke nature through form, texture, and color, without stinting on comfort or high style. Street level spots include the Whiskey Blue Bar, the Cool Juice stand (opening to both the street and the lobby), and the Oasis bar. The lobby lounge offers airy, light-drenched spaces, with 22-foot (6.6-meter) ceilings, generous volumes, and "forest wall" windows of mosaic tile. Details bring in the woods with a sense of style—and humor: "tree stumps" with backgammon or chess boards inscribed on top, floor lamps whose poles divide into branches, and walls and windows decorated with collages of leaves, plants, vegetables, seed pods, and other organic matter. Columns have been draped with fabric decorated with natural imagery, while glass is deployed in multiple colors, textures, and finishes. Materials include kota stone flooring, schist counters, hammered limestone, patinated bronze, ash, oak, and many other finishes and textures, all knit into an organic, soothing whole. The effect is calming yet exhilarating, as might be expected in an environment that offers a glimpse of the hotel's destination restaurant, Heartbeat, through a waterfall cascading down a glass wall. Other public spaces include a second-floor ballroom with a double-height ceiling, five second-floor meeting rooms with state-of-the-art audiovisual systems, and a spacious fourth-floor spa. This urbane version of "nature" has been refined and rearranged to serve the human need for aesthetic pleasure.

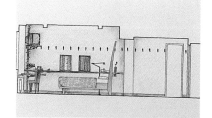  

The guestrooms and suites range from 280-square-foot (25.2 square-meter) single rooms, classified as standard or signature, up to 700-square foot (63-square-meter) suites. The signature rooms stand out by virtue of having the bed placed in the center of the room. The beds feature patinated brass headboards evocative of a garden trellis; each is graced with an oval cutout that opens on a view of the cityscape immediately upon entry into the room. Other unique guestroom amenities include window boxes of edible wheatgrass, and fine percale sheets decorated with silk-screened aphorisms in an upbeat mode, ranging from "walk with confidence" to "sleep with angels."

The W Hotels—more are to come in many U.S. cities—are owned by Starwood, whose chief Berry Sternlicht and his wife coined the name, to stand for warm, witty, wonderful, and welcoming. The W New York is all that and more, thanks in large measure to the work of the Rockwell Group.

◇ Detailed drawing of guestrooms show how carefully planned and well-thought out the rooms were in advance. Every single element has been envisioned and described both visually and in words.

◇ Photo of a guest room, with the bed moved away from the wall into the middle of the room, and an oval cutout providing a view through the patinated bronze headboard. Stenciled leaves and other organic forms enhance the connection with nature.

◇ View of guest suites and the lobby display the warmth of organic, natural colors and forms, countered by panoramic vistas onto the busy streets of midtown Manhattan.

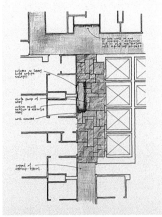

⊗ View from the mezzanine down into the light, high-ceilinged lobby, finished in soothing natural colors and furnished with comfortable seating, counterpointed with unique items like the tree stump backgammon and chess boards.

⊗ A view of the reception desk, positioned at the end of the "garden wall" featuring a collage of seeds, pods, leaves, grasses, and other organic materials.

⊗ Stone floors and wheatgrass in boxes add "organic" touches to a lobby level restroom. The glass cutouts in the windows, irregularly positioned, feature embedded leaves, another "natural" touch.

the edmond meany hotel

NBBJ

Seattle Washington

Located in Seattle's University district, the Edmond Meany first opened in 1931; the recent renovation combined restoration with replication of art deco motifs to create a fresh interpretation of 1930s style for the millennium.

Drawings of the tower exterior and a southern elevation show the architect's intent, carried out in the renovation. Exterior elevation reveals art deco details.

When it opened in 1931 the Meany Hotel quickly became a nationally recognized landmark, renowned for its innovative concrete slab construction—and for the spirited style that landed it a place on a national architectural exhibition on art deco design in 1938. Sixty-plus years had taken their toll, however, and by the mid-1990s the 159-guestroom, eighteen-story tower—for decades the tallest building in North Seattle—had fallen on hard times, victim of numerous insensitive renovations and other indignities. And so, what the NBBJ design team accomplished for the Starwood Lodging Corporation "was not a restoration but a transformation—an effort to recapture and replicate the Art Deco spirit of the building in a new form," designer Rysia Suchecka notes.

The project began with research, as the designers spent hours poring over old newspaper and magazine articles about the hotel, as well as poking around, under, and through walls, carpets, floors, and ceilings, in search of original finishes—seeking "the bones" of the hotel, says Suchecka. In the public spaces, they discovered original columns buried behind walls, a 20-foot-high (6-meter-high) ceiling hidden behind low, dingy ceiling panels, and a beautiful terrazzo floor with a pattern uncannily similar to the floor pattern they had designed to replace the dingy carpeting and layers of flooring that covered the original. As Suchecka notes, "The design process

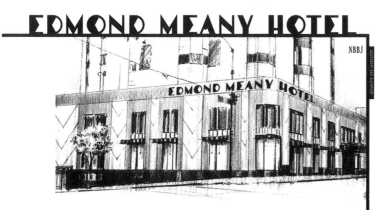

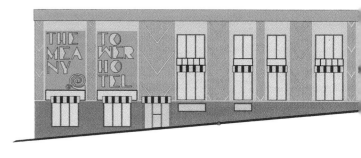

◎ Drawn prior to discovery of the original terrazzo floor, this vision of the lobby included a floor that turned out to be quite similar to the original.

◎ The designers peeled back layers of carpet and flooring to discover (and restore) the original terrazzo floor. They also removed a low ceiling, opening up the original 20-foot (6-meter) lobby ceilings, and removed walls to reveal grand columns that had been buried in previous remodels. New furnishings and lighting fixtures evoke the art deco era, but the look is clearly contemporary.

◎ Lobby level plan. The entry and lobby cross from right to center, with the zig-zag band of dark terrazzo floor. Registration is directly below the entrance, with the news café and breakfast room at bottom, meeting rooms at top, and the ballroom at left.

was responsive to the various surprises found during the demolition and construction process. As the physical building began to reveal itself, the design team discovered just how much had been concealed by the numerous remodels. We found materials that could be used, and made the necessary modifications." They also found the details to inspire the new design, a contemporary interpretation of the original style that instills in patrons "a sense of being somewhere as opposed to a sense of being anywhere," notes Suchecka.

In the public areas, the designers restored the original terrazzo floor and re-created the original lobby plan. Existing motifs and materials were refurbished and re-used where possible; new elements were designed to work with the originals. New features include custom light sconces, a two-story-tall mirror, metal work, and new furnishings, all combined to create a grand lobby that also works as an event space or cocktail lounge. The designers added a news café at the lobby level, mingling art deco motifs from the old hotel with new elements, creating a destination for hotel guests as well as university students from the neighborhood—a "fresh spirit for young types," in Suchecka's words. Metal screens evoke original details, while a concrete bar top and perforated brass bar front bring in a more contemporary sense of materials. The designers also created a new second-floor restaurant, a ballroom, several meeting rooms, a business center, and an exercise room.

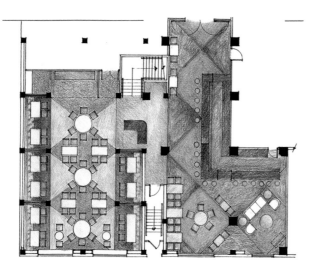

⌃ Floor plan and color sketch of the second floor restaurant.

⌃ The lobby now holds a news café, providing a destination for hotel guests and students from the neighboring university. The metal work is inspired by the original art deco style of the hotel, but the concrete counter-tops and other elements add a lively, contemporary edge. Built-in fixtures, such as the cigar cabinet, also offer an intriguing synthesis of 1930s style with contemporary flair.

⌃ The news café in an early version. The finished product is actually somewhat livelier and more dynamic in style.

Designed for the business traveler, new guestrooms feature large work desks, and corner windows with views from every room. The neutral palette provides a backdrop for the views, and for the rich red fabric on the lounge chair as well as the cherry wood furniture. All the furniture and light fixtures were custom-designed for the hotel.

⊙ Typical guestroom floor plan for the fourth through ninth floors, with guestrooms surrounding the elevator and service core. The "corn on the cob" shape of the building provides every room with a corner view.

⊙ These drawings of a guestroom and details of custom-designed lamps were done in advance of demolition and construction. A comparison with the finished photos shows that the designers pretty much stuck to their original plan for the project.

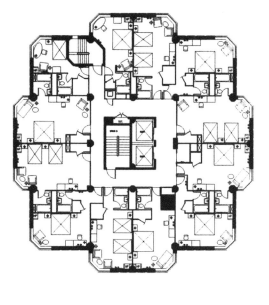

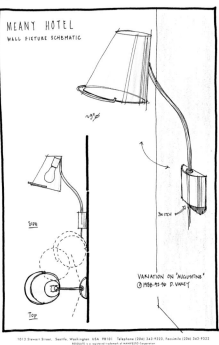

MEANY HOTEL
WALL FIXTURE SCHEMATIC

~9"∅

SIDE

SWITCH

VARIATION ON "AUGUSTINE"
© 1988-92-96 D. VAREY

TOP

1013 Stewart Street, Seattle, Washington USA 98101   Telephone (206) 343-9323, Facsimile (206) 343-9322
RESOLUTE is a registered trademark of MANIFESTO Corporation

The guestrooms were completely redone, with an eye to the comforts of extended-stay professionals. Amenities include spacious desks, wired for fax and computer. Every room offers a corner view, framed and enhanced by the neutral palette. Custom furniture, lighting, and fabrics celebrate the hotel's heritage in a contemporary interpretation, with rich cherry wood, luminescent charcoal laminate, and red lounge chair upholstery providing contrast with the more neutral backdrop tones. The artwork, selected from the archives at the nearby University of Washington, celebrates the university neighborhood of the 1930s, the era of the hotel's construction. The Meany embraces the best of its own past, elegantly integrated into a charming contemporary hotel.

⊙ Elevations and sections were done to test color schemes and scales in various parts of the hotel.

MEANY
TOWER
HOTEL

SECTION

INTERIOR SECTION

SECTION

chelsea millennium hotel

DESIGN BY PHILIPPE STARCK; INTERIOR ARCHITECTURE AND DESIGN BY DILEONARDO INTERNATIONAL

London, United Kingdom

An early sketch of the new lobby area, with new elements including the mirrors, left, reception desk, right, and carpeting, foreground, already penciled in.

A collaborative effort resulted in the creation of sleek, chic reception areas in this celebrated London property, located on fashionable Sloane Street and renowned as one of the hot new hotels on the London scene. DiLeonardo's designers worked on the hotel's two entrances, each with a canopy, as well as on completely remodeling and refurbishing the lobby and reception areas, the coffee bar, and the rest of the ground floor public spaces, including the grand staircase designed by Philippe Starck, which has emerged as the brash, attention-catching symbol of the hotel.

DiLeonardo's interiors work is intended to frame and emphasize the steel facades and the Starck staircase, which lies directly beneath a glass dome in the hotel's three-story atrium. The brash, showy staircase replaced a swimming pool that previously served as a focal point for gatherings, but was rarely used for swimming. Golden plush wall fabric, with matching gold paint from Ralph Lauren, gives off a gleam reflected in a trio of oversized floor-to-ceiling gold-framed mirrors. Black granite floors and reception desks, flecked with tiny specks of gold, sparkle in natural light by day, and in the light from custom-designed, jewel-like wall lamps in the evening, softly contrasting with claret-toned furnishings. Original fashion plates by Rene Grau announce the hotel's prime location in the midst of a celebrated array of fashionable boutiques. A custom-designed oval carpet adds another striking touch.

Views of the newly remodeled and refurbished lobby and reception desk by DiLeonardo International and Philippe Starck. The floors and desk are made of black granite flecked with gold. The staircase, designed by Starck, replaces a swimming pool. A trio of gold-framed mirrors reflect gold Ralph Lauren paint, lending a rich, warm tone to the sleek, lively interiors. Furnished with oversized armchairs, the Espresso Bar and Pavilion Lounge have been integrated into the reception lobby. The oval-shaped custom carpet adds another lively, dramatic touch.

CANOPY SKETCHES

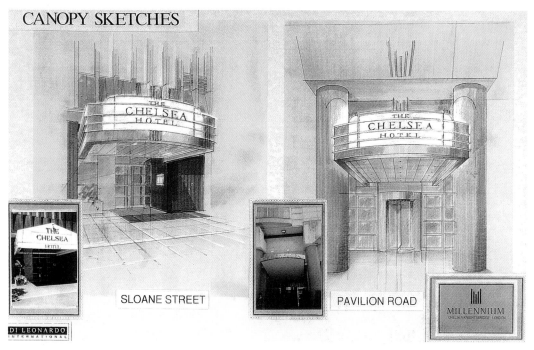

SLOANE STREET

PAVILION ROAD

⊘ Renderings of the new canopies designed by DiLeonardo
for the hotel's two entrances, on Sloane Street and Pavilion
Road. The old canopies can be seen in the smaller images.

⊘ An early sketch of a new canopy and entrance.

⊘ A more detailed canopy and entrance sketch, with specifications for materials and sizing.

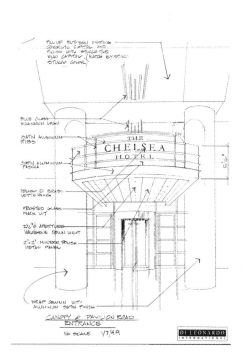

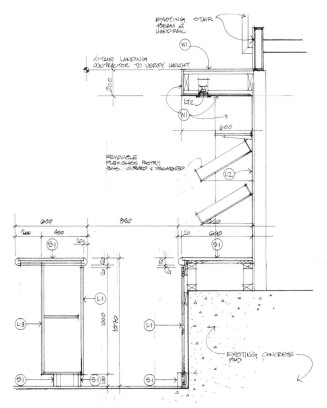

The Espresso Bar and the Pavilion Lounge, furnished with oversize armchairs, have been incorporated into the open lobby and reception area, serving not only coffees and teas but also providing food service throughout the day. The Chelsea Restaurant on the first floor offers a minimalist contrast to the warm, dark finishes of the lobby and reception areas, while the adjacent Chelsea Bar counterpoints the dining room with warm wood flooring and vivid colors in the art and furnishings. Starck and DiLeonardo have crafted a stunning, fashionable original in the heart of upscale London.

⊗ A detailed section of the Espresso Bar.

⊘ A rendering of the Espresso Bar, located beneath the stair.

VIEW A

DI LEONARDO
INTERNATIONAL

MILLENNIUM
CHELSEA KNIGHTSBRIDGE · LONDON

avalon hotel

RENOVATION DESIGN BY KONING EIZENBERG ARCHITECTURE;

INTERIOR DESIGN BY KELLY WEARSTLER

Beverly Hills, California

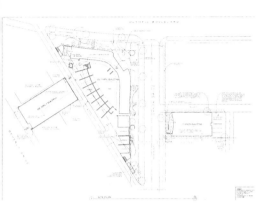

Plan shows how the three buildings relate, and also illustrates how landscaping was used to help unify the separate structures.

For most of us, the phrase Fifties Modern conjures an archetypal design image, comprised of kidney-shaped pools and coffee tables, aqua blues and greens, long, low-slung chairs and cars, Rat Pack attitude and LA light. The look went away in the late 1960s and 1970s; but more recently has returned with a welcome vengeance, for Fifties Modern has undeniable, decade-spanning cool.

At a glance some might consider L.A.'s Avalon Hotel, formerly the Beverly Carlton, a retro rerun of '50s chic, too hip to survive its own grand re-opening. A closer look reveals that the designers of the hotel—architects from the office of Koning Eizenberg working with interior designer Kelly Wearstler—have made, or re-made, a modern classic, deftly blending the best of '50s with smart, functional architecture circa 2000.

Organizing the reinvented Avalon posed some unusual problems for the designers, for like its predecessor the hotel inhabits three separate buildings: the first, on Olympic Boulevard, constructed in 1948; the second, on Canon Drive, from 1953; and the third, on Beverly Drive, from 1962. The Canon Drive wing was constructed as an apartment block, then became part of the hotel; the three buildings operated together as the Beverly Carlton for decades. The hotel claims a small share of Hollywood history as well: Marilyn Monroe lived

Drawing shows the hotel's three separate buildings, with the Olympic building at center, the Beverly building at right rear, and the Canon building at left.

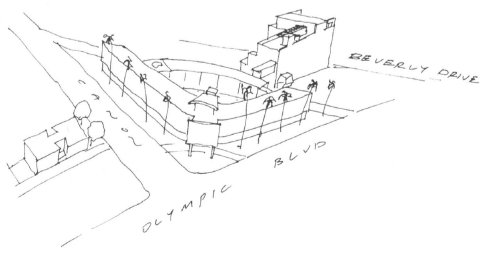

Drawing shows the new wooden louver bridge (over an alley) linking the Olympic building at left with the Beverly building at right. The new elevator container is just left of the bridge.

Existing ground floor plan of the Olympic building (prior to renovation), where the hotel's primary public spaces are located, and where the most significant architectural work was done.

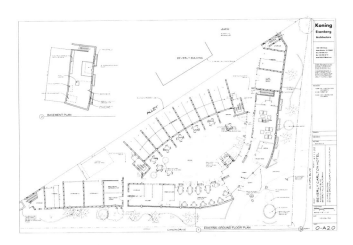

in Room 305 for two years, and Lucy and Ricky Ricardo checked in on several episodes of *I Love Lucy*. Yet things had gone downhill in recent years, until the present owners took over in 1997, and commissioned Wearstler to plan the renovation. Wearstler immediately recognized the need for an architect, and turned to the Koning Eizenberg to organize a master plan as well as collaborate with her firm, KWID, on conceptual design.

The new wave of successful boutique hotels started by Ian Schrager, Andre Balazs, and others exerted a powerful influence on the designers as they planned the renovation. These entrepreneurs recognize the value of style, but they never sacrifice comfort or a welcoming atmosphere for the sake of trendiness. And so the Avalon's new look celebrates the retro-chic cool of the '50s and '60s, but the ambience is relaxed, casually comfortable, not in the least intimidating or stiffly over-designed.

With streets, alleys, and differing architectural styles separating the three buildings, the architects' initial challenge lay in establishing the three as one entity, a single hotel. To link them visually, the designers painted

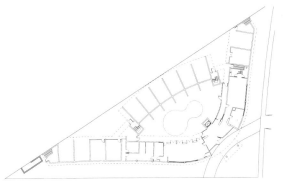

Before and after ground floor plans of the Olympic building. The most significant move was to take the elevator out and replace solid walls with glass, creating a visual link between the lobby and pool. In the new plan the restaurant lies to the left of the main entry, the lounge area and reception desk to the right.

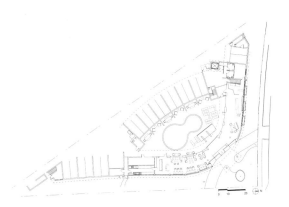

all three a seafoam green. They stripped away awnings, French doors, and other modifications that tended to clutter the structures. Out front of the entry façade of the Olympic building that contains the main lobby and forty-six guestrooms, they replaced a damaged cement tile mural with a newly designed one made of glass tiles. They expanded the lobby and dining area, opening up views to the pool by moving the elevator and installing curving glass walls in place of solid ones. A new blue terrazzo floor now flows from the lobby out towards the pool; in the lobby and adjoining restaurant, vintage '50s furnishings comfortably blend with a new copper-topped rosewood reception desk and custom-designed banquettes and coffee tables. Relocating the elevator to a position at the side and rear of the building, they enclosed it in a sculpted container, a copper-clad form that adds a powerful contemporary counterpoint to the period style—and challenges the universally-accepted blandness of elevator shafts, no matter the era or style.

The Beverly building, housing twenty-six guestrooms across an alley, was linked to the main Olympic building with a new bridge. Wooden sun control louvers and landscaping on the street side spruced up the building's appearance, while a new metal trellis and patio partitions were added on the south side. The two-story Canon

The designers created a new mural of glass tiles to replace a damaged one in front of the hotel's main building on Olympic Boulevard, and painted all three buildings in a seafoam green. The cool, retro-chic look and feel of the project dates from the 1950s. The hotel's three separate buildings date from 1948, 1953, and 1962. The signage, too, has a '50s look.

The architect designed this striking copper-clad container for a new elevator shaft toward the rear to one side of the building.

Lobby furnishings include a lounging area with vintage 1950s seating, purchased in Paris. Interior designer Kelly Wearstler created the rosewood coffee table in the foreground and the reception counter at the rear. Bamboo poles make an unusual partial screen to create a suggestion of separation between lounge and reception.

building, the smallest of the three with just 16 guestrooms, was treated with a new canopy and a new bamboo and tropical plant-lined entry ramp by landscape designer Mia Lehrer.

With twenty-eight different floor plans distributed among the eighty-eight guestrooms, interior designer Wearstler employed a common palette of cool colors and natural fabrics to establish a shared image. The palette is appropriate to the '50s style—and also helps make the rooms literally cool, refuges from the streets of oft-hot L.A. In specifying furnishings Wearstler mixed custom contemporary pieces she designed herself with classics from the '50s, then added abstracted architectural photos of the original hotel building or vintage paintings to enliven the rooms. These furnishings and accessories were specified to create an apartment-like quality—not so difficult to accomplish given that many of the guestrooms come equipped with kitchens and/or separate dining rooms, and others have semi-enclosed patios, features more often found in apartments rather than hotels. With elegant linens and down bedding in every room, in this coolly contemporary hotel guests rest assured that the '50s never looked—or felt—better.

A penthouse in the Beverly building includes a private patio furnished with an eclectic assemblage of vintage furnishings.

le merigot beach hotel and spa

DILEONARDO INTERNATIONAL, INC.

Santa Monica, California

Exterior views show the building in its sunny, Santa Monica beachfront locale. The design is cleanly contemporary, yet also evokes L.A.'s Modernist-influenced Mediterranean style.

With its balmy climate and sea-scented breezes, Santa Monica, California, has been compared to the French Riviera for decades, and many hotels, apartments, and private residences in the Southern California seaside town feature designs based on French and Spanish Mediterranean influences. Designed by Robert DiLeonardo and a team from DiLeonardo International, Le Merigot Beach Hotel and Spa, a new, 175-room hotel overlooking the Pacific in Santa Monica, displays the casual yet cosmopolitan style that signifies classic Mediterranean design.

Travelers initially will be drawn to the hotel by the lively canopy and signage—important elements in one of greater Los Angeles' few real pedestrian-friendly towns. DiLeonardo's Southern California take on Mediterranean style begins in the lobby, where artworks recall the European masters. Oversized furniture and iron lighting fixtures lend a sense of classical, old world (beachfront) style, counterpoint to the soft, clean lines and neutral backdrop of granite floors and wood-clad columns. Beyond the entry lobby, a window wall provides a panoramic Pacific view, and eases the transition to an outdoor balcony, an element inspired by the region's mellow climate. A bar adds another place for guests to linger in the lobby.

The lobby counterpoints clean, neutral backdrops of wood and painted walls with an eclectic variety of casual furnishings, and more richly detailed metalwork and alabaster panels in the mezzanine railing and especially in the custom light fixtures.

The hotel's dining rooms include the casual Café Promenade, named for the wonderful walking park across the street; and Cezanne, a dining room designed in the style of a fine French restaurant, linked to the overall project program via the use of warm-toned wood columns and iron lighting fixtures.

DiLeonardo's emphasis here lies in the guestrooms, with their canny balance of upscale, amenities-rich comfort and state-of-the-art technology. Designed to appeal above all to the international business traveler, the guestrooms feature expansive desks, oversize lounge chairs, and complete telecommunications connections.

The facility also offers a complete spa for guests, with a eucalyptus steam room, redwood sauna, a workout room, and salon for facials and other treatments. The spa helps establish the hotel as a luxury class international hotel, one that would be welcome on the French Riviera as well as the Santa Monica Riviera.

The quiet palette of the lobby extends into the casual, three meal café, where a lively Mediterranean mural makes explicit the connection with the hotel's inspiration, the French Riviera.

Spacious guestrooms and suites maintain the understated palette, but the furnishings have been specified with business travelers in mind; hence the work desk with a view.

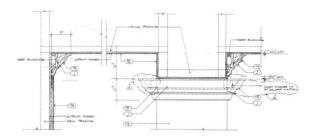

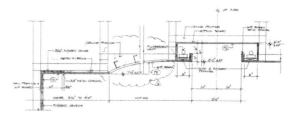

From the point of view of process, the designers were able to create renderings of the proposed spaces to explain the scheme to the clients. A comparison of renderings and completed space makes clear, once again, the expertise designers have—and must have—at creating realistic two-dimensional visions of rooms well in advance of building them. Another set of drawings reveals some of the behind-the-scenes technical challenges involved in actually creating the designs of various elements ranging from ceilings to canopies.

⊘ Two sections show the specifications for the design of the ceilings in the dining room and the boardroom, with accommodation for various lighting fixtures and other details.

⊘ A detail drawing shows the handrail designed for the mezzanine overlooking the lobby.

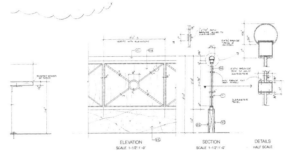

ELEVATION
SCALE 1-1/2":1'-0"

SECTION
SCALE 1-1/2":1'-0"

DETAILS
HALF SCALE

⊘ Renderings of the lobby, fine dining room, and meeting room, all completed
⊘ prior to construction, faithfully reveal the designs to come.

⊗ Richer details such as crown moldings, opulent, custom-designed lighting
⊘ fixtures (replicating those in the lobby), and plush furnishings lend the high
end restaurant, bar and private dining room a more lavish ambience.

⊗ A banquet room offers its own take on the Santa Monica Riviera.

club incognito

GISELA STROMEYER
Zurich, Switzerland

For Club Incognito, Gisela Stromeyer completely transformed a utilitarian box into a magical realm, layered with cloud-like forms that create a sense of fun and fantasy, a dream world of a nightclub. Stromeyer's design reflects her background as a professional dancer, and one can certainly see the fluid grace of body movement in the wonderfully taut, sculpted forms she creates out of tensile fabrics. When Stromeyer turned from dance to design, studying architecture in Germany and then at the Pratt Institute in New York City, she followed in the footsteps of a family of tentmakers, including her father Peter Stromeyer, who with partner Otto Frei expanded the use of tensile forms into dramatic, large-scale projects. (Frei's and Stromeyer's most memorable tensile structures were those they created for the 1967 Montreal World's Fair and the Munich Olympics in 1972.) While Gisela Stromeyer's work has not yet reached that scale, after apprenticing with the New York tensile specialist architecture firm FTL she formed her own business and soon carved out a niche as a maker of stunningly graceful, elegant tensile structures in myriad applications including retail stores, showrooms, offices, museums, residences—and nightclubs, such as the Club Incognito.

Stromeyer's commission in Zurich came about when the club's owner visited New York City in search of ideas and furniture. He saw Stromeyer-designed lighting fixtures at a retail store, tracked her down, and asked her to come to Zurich to design the club. Upon accepting the commission, Stromeyer traveled to Zurich to inspect the

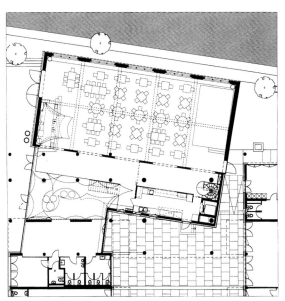

Floor plan shows the basic utilitarian box shape of the club, with Stromeyer's constructions softening up the grid in the area at center left, not far from the club entrance at bottom left.

SKETCH OF ENTRANCE AREA SOMETHING LIKE THIS!

Stromeyer worked with an architectural plan, photos she shot on a brief site visit, and her own sketches, one of the entry and another of the overall space from a couple of angles, when making the designs for her fabric structures.

site, a structure located in an old riverfront warehouse district currently undergoing gentrification. The old/new structure itself included a circa-nineteenth-century warehouse linked by a double-height skylit entry hall to a recent addition of concrete and glass. Stromeyer walked through the building, began conceptualizing her design even as she photographed the site—"my ideas come as a response to the flow, the shape, the ceiling heights, and the location of the entrance," she says— and returned to her studio in New York. She developed her final designs using these sketches, her photographs, and a detailed architectural plan, complete with precise measurements that she obtained from the owner.

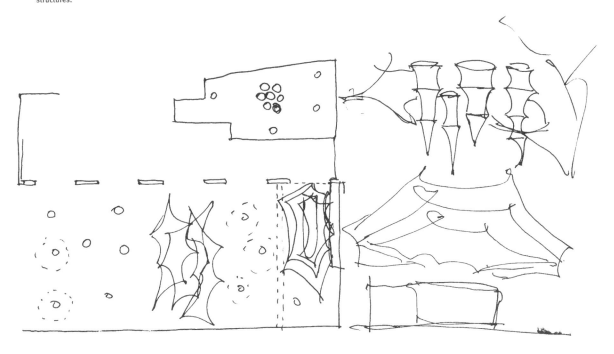

The club owner developed the basic organization of
space: the ground floor is open space, half of it devoted
to table seating and the bar, with a stage at the far end
of the room for performances and fashion events. A second bar and lounge on a mezzanine level offer views
down into the theater area. Without altering the basic
concrete box, Stromeyer utterly transformed this utilitarian envelope, installing layered waves of ethereal
white Spandex forms to counterpoint the existing building's material toughness and solidity—and to organize
space and scale down the volume. The designer says,
"This is a different way of thinking about design,
because the fabric can be worked into three-dimensional
shapes; it has more life to it. You pull it one way and influence something else. The material is very responsive."

Stromeyer's work begins in the foyer, where she installed
three horizontal, sail-like elements that wrap around a
cluster of five suspended, column-shaped forms lit from
within. To bring focus to the bar area, she crowned it
with a canopy of layered, tautly stretched fabric panels.
In each area, the sculpted complexity of the forms plays
off the simplicity of the enclosing box, and the clean,
simple whiteness of the fabric as well. The white fabric
also serves as a vehicle for color: colored lamps can be
fitted inside the structures so that they glow from within, and the curving white forms also work as blank can-
vases for colored light projections sent from theater fixtures. A lighting designer did the installation at

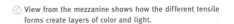
View from the mezzanine shows how the different tensile forms create layers of color and light.

Incognito, with recommendations on the illumination plan from Stromeyer, who created the internal lighting for the suspended "column" forms. With the capacity to change gels and lamp colors, the interior palette remains completely flexible.

As per their usual working methods, Stromeyer and staff made the pieces themselves, shaping, cutting, and sewing stock or custom-made fabric to fit based on her observations of the space. She didn't go back until final installation, when she installed the pieces herself, using lengths of wire to shape the material and anchor it to hooks in the walls, floors, and ceilings. The only other "structural" components in the Incognito installation are the metal hoops inside the five suspended pieces, which are open on top to ventilate the built-in lights.

Views show the evocative, otherworldly forms, lit by theater projector lights or from within, floating against various backdrop walls and curtains. The horizontal forms attach to the wall with hooks, while the vertical forms are suspended by wires.

next door nobu

ROCKWELL GROUP
New York, New York

Rockwell quickly assembled all the components, including a model, bottom, and multiple images and textures, to explain his concept for the restaurant.

Floor plan, with entry at top left, curving sushi bar at top center, kitchen at right. The service bar or "sake temple" is at bottom center.

Some might call it overkill, putting a second, similar restaurant right next door to a much-loved original; but when the parties involved include Nobuyaki Matsuhisa, Drew Nieporent, and Robert DeNiro, and the designer is David Rockwell and his Rockwell Group, confidence bred of success overcomes all doubt. And so we have Next Door Nobu, next door to the fabulously successful Nobu in trendy Tribeca, downtown Manhattan. Inspiration for the hipper, more casual, no-reservations-required Next Door Nobu came from the original Nobu, and from another, quirkier source: the Japanese movie Tampopo, featuring what David Rockwell describes as the world's most perfect, always-been-there Japanese noodle shop.

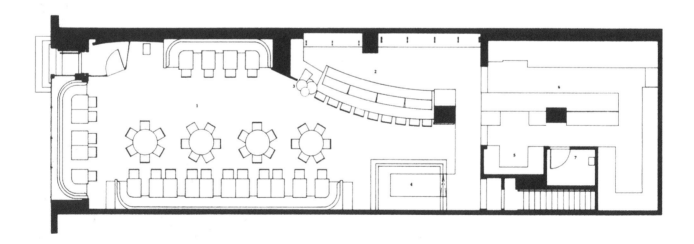

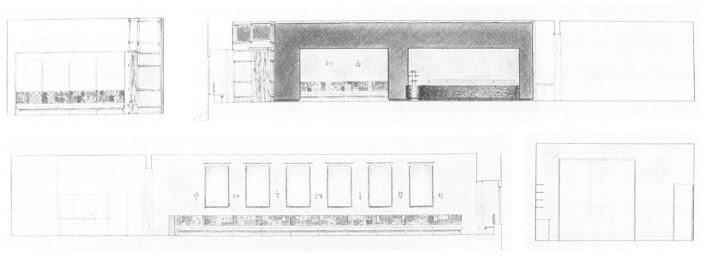

⊗ Four directional elevation drawings show the banquette seating, with colorful
fabric, beneath the six tatami mats on the east, south, and north walls. The
south elevation also shows the Yakinori finished wall, and the sushi bar at
right.

Next Door Nobu, tucked into a 2,000-square-foot (180-
square-meter) shoebox-shaped interior (1300-square-
feet of dining room), borrows a few elements from big
brother next door, not least of which is a sense of play-
fulness. This quality is perhaps most obviously
expressed in Next Door Nobu's sake temple, a glowing,
translucent cube lined with shelves of silhouetted sake
bottles, at the rear of the dining room. (On a practical
note, it screens the service bar.) Thonet dining chairs
and scorched ash and river rock detailing are also
reprised from Nobu, but in spite of the Nobu connection the new seventy-seat restaurant has its own
distinctive style, a graceful orchestration of subtly
amusing surprises against a serenely appealing backdrop. Just inside the entry, a gently curving, dark green
wall glows luminously, its finish composed of yakinori,
or dried seaweed, specially treated and sealed with lacquer. The perimeter walls feature a soft straw tone,
achieved by hand-rubbing Venetian plaster; decorations
include a trio of 4 by 7 foot (1.2 by 2.1 meter) woven
tatami mats that serve as wall hangings, their appealingly organic texture and color offering counterpoint to
the multi-colored quilted velvet fabrics covering the
banquettes along the dining room's two longer walls.

Unusual textures and surprising objects and details add enormously to Next Door Nobu's richness. Stock laminate flooring looks pleasantly worn, like old steel or concrete. The ceiling finish was inspired, literally, by noodles (and by the addition of noodle specialty dishes to the menu). Lighting fixtures suspended from the ceiling have been made from old woven Japanese fishing baskets. At one end of the dining room's sushi bar, resting atop a cylindrical base of river stones—a nod to the original Nobu—a trio of hammered woks attached to a rotating armature display fresh seafood atop mounds of crushed ice. Small, subtle inlays of mother of pearl add luster to the walls, while playful mosaics brighten the restrooms.

Next Door Nobu was assembled quickly on a small budget, with little advance planning. The color elevations and sample boards drawn up by the designers gave the owners a clue as to what to expect, but essentially, having worked with David Rockwell on several other successful projects, the owners trusted him enough to give him free rein. Next Door Nobu's lively, entertaining interiors suggest they made the right decision.

A trio of hammered woks on a rotating armature serves as a seafood display at one end of the sushi bar. The woks rest upon a cylindrical base of river stones—a motif Rockwell used first in the original Nobu.

⌃ Silhouetted sake bottles emptied by patrons of the original Nobu make a lively graphic decorative element, lined up on backlit shelves built into two walls that screen the service bar. The scorched ash bartop and the hammered wok seafood display occupy the foreground.

⌄ The designers transformed old Japanese fishing baskets into beautiful, unique light fixtures.

⌃ Detail of banquette section, fish basket lantern, and tatami mat flanked by mother of pearl inlays eloquently illustrates the aesthetic richness achieved by the careful arrangement of these simple yet subtly compelling elements.

⌄ Detail of the lustrous green wall that curves in from the entry. The wall is made of specially treated and lacquered sheets of yakinori, or dried seaweed.

ideya restaurant

PNB DESIGN
New York City

⊗ The uneven walls were painted white at the bar and the refrigerated vitrine adds to the market image.

Latin American cuisine is the current rage in New York City's SoHo, and with it comes various manifestations of exuberant vernacular design. For Ideya Restaurant, PNB turned to the vibrant imagery of Latin American markets and shops, yet cleansed the visual palette with hard crisp lines and white walls.

The design direction evolved from the owner's desire to "create an environment different from the other themed restaurants in New York City, which are sometimes overwhelming," the designers say. The strategy developed by the designers focused on a few simple elements relating to open markets and bodegas, while the owners concentrated on developing a menu based on a new interpretation of traditional Latin American dishes. The owners also requested a flexible design for the 60-seat dining room, suitable for different venues from Sunday brunch to weekday dinner to after-hours lounge.

PNB partners Bill Peterson and Carol Swedlow began by simply whitewashing the uneven and crumbling walls of the 1,200-square-foot (108-square-meter) interior to create a neutral background. In that shell, they inserted a 32-foot-long (9.6 meter-long) banquette, a streamlined modern fixture upholstered in polypropylene lawn chair webbing, reminiscent of open market seating or backyard barbecue chairs. The sleek banquette is meant to recall "dad's pork chops" or the "freshest produce."

⊗ Made of polypropylene lawn-chair webbing, the main banquette stretches 32 feet (9.6 meters) and is the defining design element. It is meant to reflect materials found in the Latin American marketplace. Mirrors sit above the banquette, with the painted panels dropped behind.

Along the wall above the banquette is a retractable, exuberantly colored mural. It's actually a mural system—four, 8-foot-long (2.4-meter-long) panels that can be alternated by means of a manually operated cable and pulley system. The panels can be switched in order or dropped behind the banquette and replaced by mirrors, and dramatically change the mood or the dining room.

Opposite the banquette, the bar is fronted with generic bathroom tiles. A freestanding refrigerated vitrine sits next to the bar at the front of the restaurant, reinforcing the bodega image. Yet, it's the small details taken from the Latin marketplace that establishes the entire ambiance—the fixtures with bare lightbulbs, the oilcloth tablecloths, the candles in glass, the simple wooden bar stools, the wall-mounted fans, the bentwood chairs, and the hanging scale.

View from the rear of the restaurant shows the mirror raised above the banquet (top) and lowered behind the banquet to reveal the decorative murals (bottom).

The restaurant's Latin American heritage is exuberantly expressed in its colorful murals.

A manually operated cable system allows the murals to be alternated with each other and the mirrors below.

rock restaurant

RIOS ASSOCIATES

Los Angeles, California

Glass walls allow passersby a vision of the interior, with its field of cloud-like globe lights. The lights and signage lend the restaurant an eye-catching street presence. The graphic intrigue of the wordbar over the bar, right, adds to the street appeal.

The ROCK Restaurant, a renovation/conversion completed by Rios Associates for Los Angeles chef Hans Rockenwagner, creates a lively, easily identifiable street-level dining room in the nondescript context of a two-story mall. Rockenwagner sought to create a second presence in L.A. that would appeal to a more mainstream clientele than his more upscale existing restaurant. At the same time, the designers had to contend with the space's previous function as a dining room for another local celebrity chef. The program also called for doubling the seating to accommodate 114 diners while figuring out a means of abating the ruinously high levels of ambient interior noise that previously existed in the space.

As is revealed in the colorful pre-construction drawings and in the photographs of the completed project, the designers from Rios elected to utilize graphic design as the key element in quickly creating a low-cost but attention-getting pop identity for the space. The graphics package was then integrated into the design of space; for example, the bar design influenced the look of the menus, while the style of the menus influenced the signage and the architectural forms inspired the patterns on the dinner plates.

wood screen and paint pattern concept

paint existing plaster

wordbar concept

painted graphics on wall

new painted pattern

new printed adhesive film on inside of existing glass

2 graphics concept

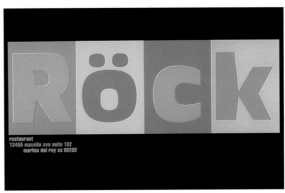

restaurant
13455 maxella ave suite 102
marina del rey ca 90292

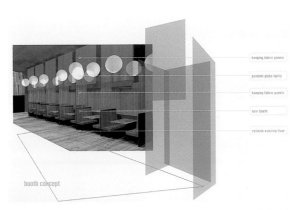

hanging fabric panels

pendant globe lights

hanging fabric panels

new booth

refinish existing floor

booth concept

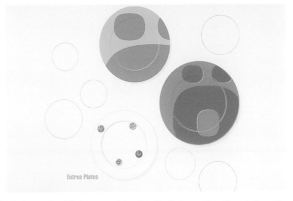

Entree Plates

Six from a series of ten drawings illustrates the interplay of graphic design, interior design, and architecture as envisioned by the designers. From the exterior wall of orange-hued vertical patterning to the wordbar over the bar, the project was seen from the beginning as a complete, multi-dimensional unity.

On the exterior, the designers created a wall of bright oranges that create a pattern-like shifting exclamation points. They wrapped this wall into the interior, where shadows and backlighting dramatize the pattern as it shifts into three dimensions, and takes on a secondary function as an acoustic baffle. In the dining room the pattern expands fully into three dimensions, and becomes a wine storage cabinet.

In its previous incarnation the space had featured an undulating ceiling; the designers painted the ceiling a deep sky blue, then suspended a profusion of 24-inch (600 millimeters) globe lights in a cloud-like field, creating a dynamic new ceilingscape that also helps with noise abatement, for the globes hang low enough to absorb sound. As a counterpoint, noise becomes image in the bar area, where a "word bar" of graphic texts (things you might hear in a barroom conversation) have floated up from the mouths of patrons to land on an overhead wall.

An exercise in lively, low-budget design, the ROCK offers a complete signature space for the client, saturated in the kind of visual pop energy that is sure to draw a crowd.

⊘ Detail of bar shows two graphic motifs—the globes, and the orange "exclamation points" in multiple hues—that find expression on a larger scale in the design of the space.

⊗ Views of the dining room from opposite perspectives. The orange-hued exterior wall becomes an acoustic wall inside— and a wine cabinet as well. Painted blue, the undulating ceiling serves as the "sky" backdrop for the clouds of light fixtures.

⊘ Tabletop details show the various graphic elements that inspire and reflect the architecture and interior design—all have been treated as a single integrated package.

postrio restaurant

DESIGN BY ENGSTROM DESIGN GROUP

Las Vegas, Nevada

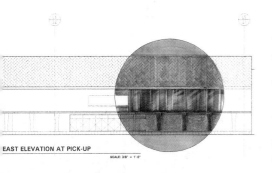

EAST ELEVATION AT PICK-UP

SCALE: 3/8" = 1'-0"

◇ Elevation drawings show different sections of the restaurant, with colors, fabrics, and materials inset for effect.

Located in the Venetian Resort-Hotel-Casino's replica of Venice's Piazza San Marco, the latest incarnation of Wolfgang Puck's Postrio offers a flamboyant blend of contemporary American and Mediterranean influences, in a style that suggests San Francisco gone Baroque. This lavish approach, which "drew on the visual character of Venice and San Francisco," note the designers, was intended to differentiate Postrio from the more contemporary, pop-oriented Southern California style of Puck's other Las Vegas restaurants such as Spago.

To enhance the Venetian ambience, the design team incorporated hand-blown glass, rich fabrics, glass-tile mosaics, and vivid, jewel-toned colors into a 11,500-square-foot (1,035-square-meter) framework of Old World-influenced architectural elements. With the work of multiple artisans neatly integrated into the interiors, the restaurant contains four distinct areas, including an informal, bistro-style café, a lively bar, a grand dining room, and a more elegant private dining room.

◇ The restaurant's "outdoor" dining room is contained by a handmade steel railing on the edge of the Venetian's replica of Piazza San Marco.

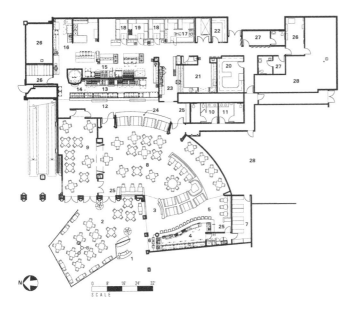

⊘ Floorplan shows "exterior" dining patio at bottom left, with the bar to the right and the main dining room and private dining room at center and left. The kitchen and a future dining room to come lie across the top in plan.

⊘ Early sketches bear a strong resemblance to the finished interiors, with curves and patterns creating a rich, Baroque-influenced atmosphere.

Located behind a hand-made steel railing along the edge of the piazza, the bistro serves as an "open-air" café (the Vegas version of Piazza San Marco is an air-conditioned interior volume) outside the dining room, with marble tables and cast aluminum chairs establishing the informal style. From here, the restaurant's rich, colorful interior entices, visible through high, classically proportioned arches. The first volume contains the bar, which serves as a transitional, exterior/interior space, richly decorated with glass tile mosaics on the bar front and the structural columns. Marble floor tiles echo the ziggurat pattern found in the Doge's Palace in Venice, in tones of amber, purple, and terracotta.

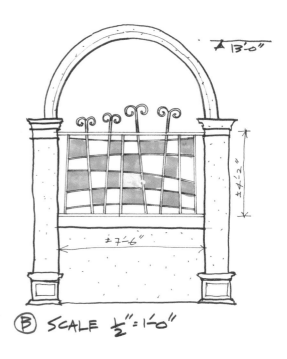

Ⓑ SCALE ½" = 1'-0"

⊘ Drawings show scale of architectural and decorative elements.

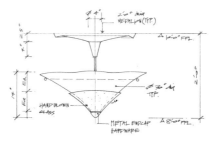

Color drawings show details and relationships while the designers were developing colors and forms.

Detail drawings of custom-designed light fixtures.

The big scale and sumptuous finishes of the main dining room evoke an Old World grand room, with large, high ceiling coffers, overscale blown-glass chandeliers, and a curving rear wall. Handmade wall coverings, textured like leather, line the walls and coffers. A decorative glass window, composed of layers of slumped, etched, and sandblasted colored glass, screens the kitchen while providing a rich central focal point. The adjacent private dining room continues the rich decorative themes found in the main dining room.

Las Vegas has reinvented itself as an amazing conglomeration of architectural and cultural fantasy—and a world-class dining destination. With Puck at the helm, the opulently-finished Postrio should soon emerge as one of Vegas' favorite dining rooms.

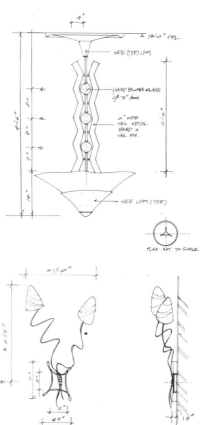

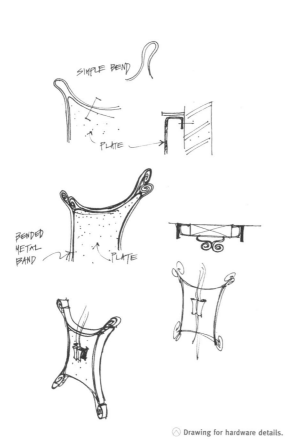

Drawing for hardware details.

Inspired by the maritime cities of Venice and San Francisco, Postrio's lavish, neo-Baroque interiors feature rich, textured finishes, warm deep colors, hand-made light fixtures, and other unique decorative elements. The columns and bar front are clad with glass-tile mosaics.

american cinematheque
at the egyptian theatre

HODGETTS + FUNG

Hollywood, California

The 1929 premier of D.W. Griffith's *Intolerance* at the Egyptian Theater, showing the theater's original courtyard and columns.

Tarnished and badly deteriorated, the splendor of the 1922 Egyptian Theatre was evident to preservationists who dreamed of its revival. Architect Hodgetts + Fung realized its survival would involve a careful renovation of its interior surfaces, adaptation of its exterior spaces, and a thorough modernization of its motion picture facilities. Only then would the 45,000-square-foot (4,050 square-meter) facility adequately provide a new home for a Los Angeles-based nonprofit viewer support film and exhibition organization, the American Cinematheque.

Over the years, renovations to the theater had hidden rather than celebrated its art deco style. The goal of Hodgetts + Fung was to restore the original processional entry forecourt to its original appearance—its walls decorated with a colorful Egyptian hieroglyph motif. Retail spaces once again line the western forecourt, as well as palm trees. Also restored is the double-height entry portico with its giant four-foot-diameter (1.2 meter-diameter) columns and ticket booth.

The splendid Art Deco details of the 1922 Egyptian Theater. The ceiling was restored to its original appearance, new acoustic paneling was added above the screen, and the steel "armature" carries HVAC equipment.

⊘ The steel "armature" allows a clear view of the historic ceiling while it holds acoustical, MEP, and lighting systems.

⊘ The original neon entrance sign was recreated.

To preserve the greatest amount of historic fabric involved the use of a holistic structural bracing system that stabilized the exiting wall. The bracing system used the existing footings and concrete shearwall systems in the sections of the existing wall, which allowed the removal of a minimum of hollow clay tile. Original lighting fixtures and the decorative fountain on the west wall were reproduced. The grandest element of the design was the restoration of the entry portico, complete with giant columns, and the original ticket booth location, thus returning the façade of the theater to the appropriately grand and impressive original design.

A state-of-the art motion picture theater was created to provide flexible presentation capabilities that would allow the showing of small-format silent films with organ accompaniment, as well as a modern, large-screen presentations with digital sound. The theater offers 400 seat for daily programming and 600 seats for special presentations.

⊘ The plan of the theater complex with the palm court leading to the theater.

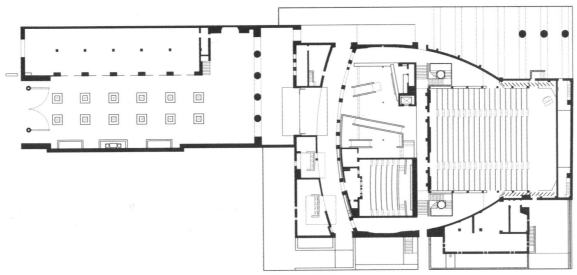

The "scarab" over the proscenium was restored to its original splendor.

Storefronts line the restored courtyard.

The Egyptian theme was renewed at the Portico.

Adjustable acoustic panels at the sidewalls can be used to create different acoustical conditions in the theater.

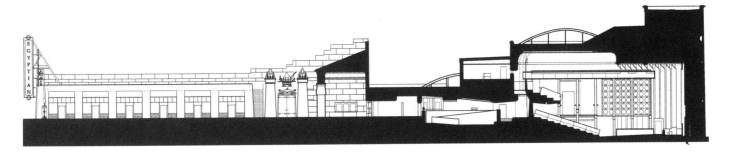

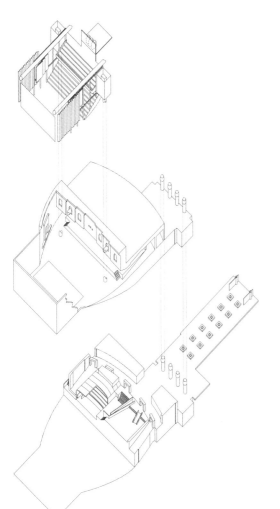

⊗ Longitudinal section shows the courtyard leading to the theater.

⊗ Axonometric reveals the steel armature.

⊗ In renovating the theater, the architect developed a storyboard.

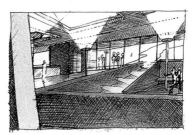

private office

CECCONI-SIMONE INC.

Toronto, Canada

Glass entrance doors open onto the lobby of the corporate office space that the clients refer to as a "jewel-like" space. The three-story atrium features an onyx-clad elevator at the rear.

To meet the client's request for a "jewel-like" environment, designers at Cecconi Simone relied on quality materials, crisp lines, natural light, and spatial drama to create a sparkling corporate office. Meticulous attention to detailing, the inclusion of custom-designed furniture and the use of warm wood bring a welcoming feeling to the interiors. In addition, the architects successfully met the goal to create "an indoor piazza, to facilitate open communication, and give the office a true sense of community."

The private offices are located within a freestanding, boutique building in which three floors surround a central courtyard. The elevator core was originally introduced as a "functional necessity" but became the "visual and social" focus of the building. To highlight that core, the designers chose to cover the wall with onyx and backlight it, so that at night it becomes a "beacon" that "unifies the space and the people within

A cappuccino bar beckons guests into the reception area.

A staircase runs the height of the three-story, atrium office building, which receives an abundance of natural light through the front façade.

Stairs with custom-designed railing leads upward through the three-story atrium space.

Windows of private offices open onto the atrium space.

Custom-designed benches made of Anigre wood dot the corridors.

it." A staircase also winds upward through the atrium, further unifying the space. The private offices that surround the atrium on all three floors have windows that open up onto the core "enhancing the piazza feel of the space." The second and third floors have an outdoor deck area to "bring the outdoor surroundings" into the office and "provide a sense of open-ness and tranquility."

A welcoming sense of community is established in the reception area. There, guests can enjoy a cappuccino at a custom-design bar and hold an impromptu meeting on a custom-designed bench. The visitor can view the staircase railings, designed by the architect, and the Eramosa limestone floor tiles and Anigre wood details that are carried into the rest of the interiors. In fact, custom workstations are designed to be accommodating but barely noticeable, to give the office a clean, symmetrical look. Lighting was very carefully designed to act as both indoor and outdoor light and to correspond with the great amount of natural light that filters into the space during the day and the light that filters through the onyx at night.

The boardroom features a custom-designed table and shelving system. The lighting system was carefully integrated with the furniture system.

The atrium as seen from the first floor.

Drawings reveal the architect's close attention to details and the inclusion of custom-designed furniture throughout the office. The custom-designs range from benches to the cappuccino bar in the lobby to the conference table in the board room to the stair railing.

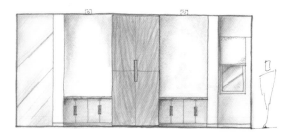

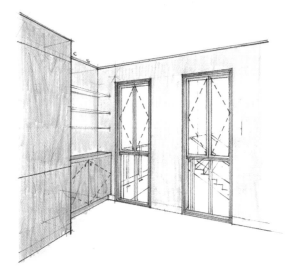

PLAN · BOARDROOM TABLE

ELEVATION – BOARDROOM TABLE

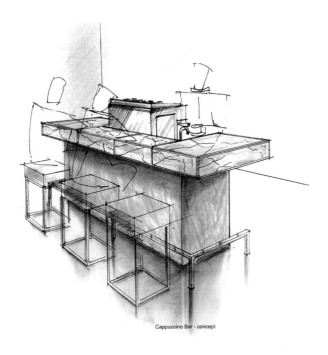

Cappuccino Bar - concept

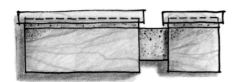

PLAN - COURTYARD BENCH

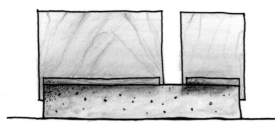

ELEVATION: COURTYARD BENCH

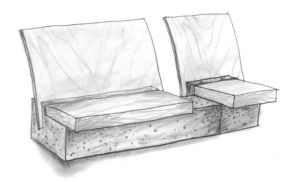

COURTYARD BENCH

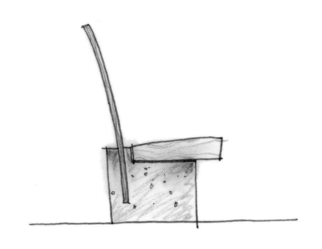

santos SAOABU (south australia & offshore australia business units tenancy)

CARR DESIGN GROUP PTY. LTD.
Adelaide, South Australia

The Carr Design Group's clean, contemporary design approach provided eight floors of sparely finished, purely functional workspace, designed to reflect, celebrate, and enhance Santos' corporate image and culture for itself and for public consumption, while also creating spaces that efficiently accommodated over 500 employees. After 40 years in the oil exploration business Santos has emerged as a major international energy producing company, headquartered in Adelaide, South Australia, with exploration facilities and production plants distributed throughout remote Outback Australia and offshore. Created by Adelaide's Carr Design Group, Santos' new interiors shown here were specified to integrate the company's South Australian and Offshore Australian Business Units into the corporate high-rise headquarters building, known as Santos House, in Adelaide. Santos is a business employing the latest technologies, and yet also one whose fieldwork is staged in the more remote realms of the natural world.

The eight floors of offices have been designed subtly to evoke the interaction of nature and technology that lies at the heart of what Santos does. In discussing the project, Vivienne Mackley, the associate in charge, says, "When walking around the existing tenancy we noticed all these fantastic aerial photographs of desert landscapes with the red and brown of the earth offset by oil refineries and pipelines. These shots helped determine our understanding of the energy business and influenced our palette. So as soon as you step out of the lift you see a clear horizon, broken up both by high-tech and natural formations—a landscape that is the heart and soul of the Santos business."

◈ Floor plans show layout of ninth floor and a generic plan. The "generic" plan, developed in advance of the real plans, indicated the general idea of putting workstations on the perimeter and meeting areas at the corners, with facilities in the core.

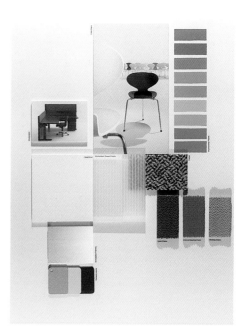

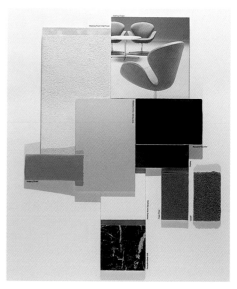

◈ Sample and color boards show palette of colors, materials, and textures for the office space and the reception area. Each has been developed as a response to the Santos business, which takes high technology into remote natural terrain.

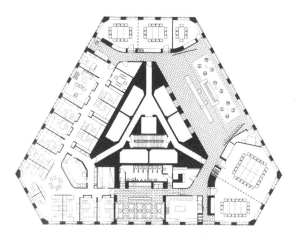

Tenth floor plan, with reception at upper right, meeting rooms at top and bottom right, and workstations along the perimeter walls, left and bottom. The reception waiting area is situated by the windows on the perimeter of the reception area at right. The Café is at center bottom.

In presenting design ideas to the client, the firm used sample and color boards intended to evoke the desert and other natural scenes. One set of samples was presented for the back offices; another for the public reception area. Drawings were also used to illuminate the designers' vision of the reception area, with its long, blocky desk floating in front of an anchoring wall of marble.

Early drawings of the reception area, with the floating aluminum desk in foreground and the cylindrical display at rear. The second image shows the end of the desk with the waiting area behind it, and the stainless steel wall that backs the cylindrical displays at far left.

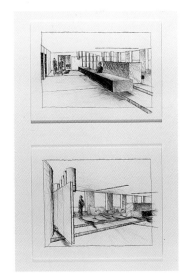

Views of the tenth floor reception area. The long aluminum reception desk floats, cantilevered, against a black, white-veined marble wall. The wall screens a waiting area furnished with Eames chairs and Saarinen tables, and a built-in banquette behind the wall. The cylinders floating against the steel wall backdrop display a history of the company.

The interaction of technology and nature inspired the palette; the building, triangular in shape, offered another kind of inspirational challenge, to organize the floor plates functionally. Each floor has been assigned a different segment of the company business, per early organizational plans developed by the designers. The reception area on the tenth floor, with its more "public" profile, provided the designers with a stage upon which to most dramatically express and affirm the corporate image. The client requested a look, says Mackley, "that would reinforce the company's image of being a major energy producer and a efficient operation, ready to take appropriate levels of risk and implement new technologies for the future benefit of the company." Seeking to avoid ostentation, the designers sought an appearance "imbued with conservatism, modesty and solidity" while still suggesting "progressive, leading edge design and technology." Thus, the cool, generous expanse of the reception area, devoid of ornamentation. To anchor the space, a black marble wall veined in white backs a long, gray reception desk of cantilevered aluminum. The wall screens an informal waiting/meeting area behind it, one step higher. This open zone has been furnished with classic Eames Soft Pad Lounge Chairs in a

desert tone, along with white marble Saarinen tables. Containing the waiting area at both ends, thick, curving, clay-colored walls carve out meeting room space. Stainless steel cantilevered blade walls define the reception zone, directing people through the triangular core to the offices beyond. Close to the elevator bays, one steel wall serves as backdrop for a corporate display installation, a history of the company inscribed on a series of aluminum cylinders.

After observing how the employees operated, the designers were actually able to reduce the number of enclosed offices, instead opting for open plan workstations situated on the perimeters of each floor, giving the general staff natural light and views with the private offices closer to the core. Workstation areas on each floor were developed as flexible modules that could be adapted to use as single workstations, single offices, or meeting rooms. To offset the difficulties of the triangular floor plan, the designers located what they call "nodal zones" at the corners: spaces configured for teamwork, with 180-degree views of the city.

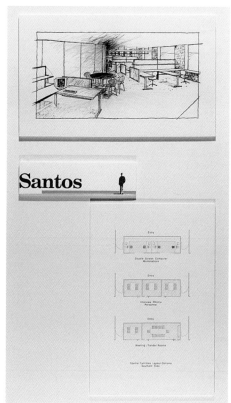

Santos

Workstation areas on the perimeter of each floor feature modular designs so that pairs of single stations can be changed into a single office, and groups of four can be made into a meeting room. Drawing shows early version of workstation zone with informal meeting areas, plus a plan that illustrates how the modular concept will work.

Thick, curving walls in clay tones enclose meeting rooms adjacent to the reception area on the tenth floor. Cutouts tend to lighten the walls. The color evokes the earth tones of the desert sites of Santos operations.

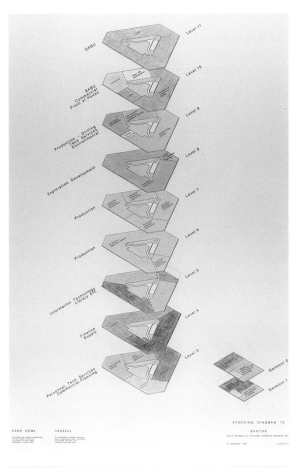

⊗ Detail shows the subtle evocation of nature through texture and tone, played off against the more slick finishes of the furnishings. This understated interaction is the essence of the design.

⊗ The in-house Oil Patch Café features custom-designed stools, and Eames chairs with walnut veneer in the dining room.

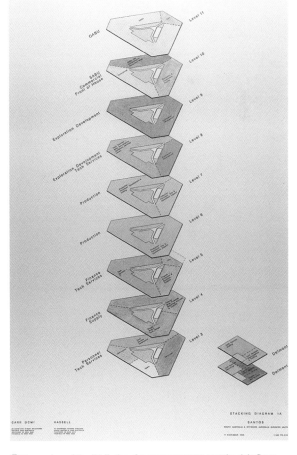

⊗ Two versions of the distribution of company segments over the eight floors show how the organization evolved from an earlier to a later plan, based on feedback from the client and other factors.

broadmoor development company

RANDY BROWN ARCHITECT

Omaha, Nebraska

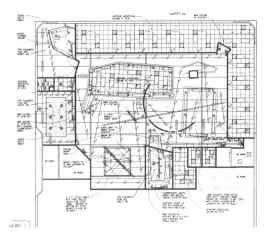

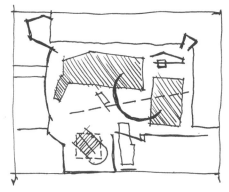

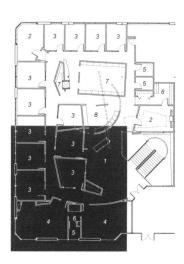

Although this project was completed on a reasonable schedule of six months—two months of design development and four months of construction—the 10,500 square feet (945 square meters) of flowing, sculpted interiors appear to reflect an almost improvisational approach to shaping space. The office spreads out over the ground and basement levels of a new building in suburban Omaha—a building not yet completed when design development began. This absence of information about the real-world look of the building actually worked to the design team's advantage, as Randy Brown notes: "With the building shell previously unseen by the clients, there were no preconceptions of the finished form."

Brown's philosophy makes a perfect match for the Broadmoor clients, given his firm's penchant for design-build, on-site architectural exploration and experimentation. The two partners that operate the Broadmoor Development Company, which builds and manages apartment and office buildings, were neither conservative nor close-minded, an approach atypically found with most developers. They wanted "a design that expressed their ideas about openness," says Brown, "one that would inspire creative thinking, and set a standard for future projects."

⊗ An early plan, and several late ones, show how Brown's vision for the space remained constant throughout the process.

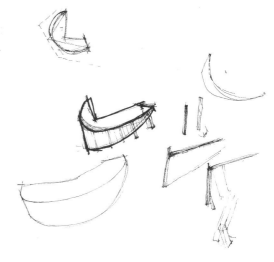

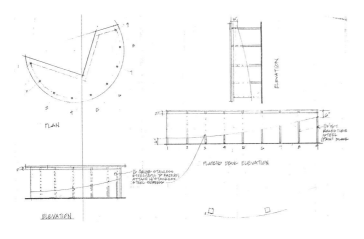

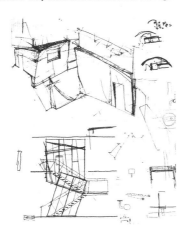

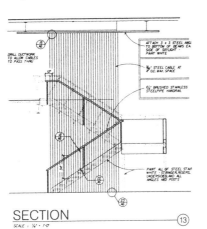

SECTION
SCALE : ½" = 1'-0"   ⑬

Granted the good fortune of open-minded clients and "no preconceptions," Brown was able to "involve the clients. We showed them what we were doing, educating them so they were involved in the whole process." That process resulted in a kinetic, dramatic interior landscape, one that Brown describes rather poetically: "Space as form...carved from the inside out. Not to be seen as walls that divide, or to be understood as constructions of common building materials. There would be just form. Foreign transformations of material. Seamless mutations of natural wood appear to have been sculpted from solid. Metal masses become oversized and endless with mechanical fasteners." The designer's notes go on in this vein, and the quotes, though somewhat abstract, serve to indicate what he is thinking about on a philosophical level while making these unusual yet ultimately functional spaces. What makes the words resonate is bouncing them off the completed design, visible here in myriad drawings, plans, and photographs. Brown's intriguing counterpoint of conceptual thinking and hands-on, do-it-yourself construction has resulted in a distinct, original, and expressive piece of work.

Broadmoor's interior finishes and furnishings have been constructed of very basic stuff: concrete, steel, wood, and glass, reflecting the company's business. Yet these materials collide, collude, and otherwise interact in all kinds of surprising ways, for example in the custom-designed reception desk that juxtaposes maple plywood horizontal planes against glasswork surfaces and vertical steel supports.

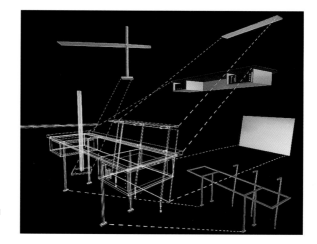

A computer-generated drawing shows the components of the reception desk in "exploded" form. The custom-designed desk juxtaposes maple, glass, and steel elements.

The partners and twelve employees work out of offices around the perimeters on each floor, with numerous meeting areas, each featuring a unique design, randomly sited throughout. These meeting areas range from glass-enclosed rooms to entirely open zones. Aside from the meeting rooms, the dynamic sense of openness and flow through the interior has been enhanced with an assortment of constructions such as stainless steel-clad objects and maple plywood planes; interior windows sited to frame views of these dynamic landscapes add to the sense of movement and action.

The only natural light in the project comes from a skylight over the main stair. Brown enhanced this limited daylight with an uplit bar joist "to make spaces glow," he says. "We also specified library lights, making them focal points by using them out of context."

In the end, notes Brown, "Form became the solution the client didn't immediately know that they pursued. The result is suitable for their real estate development offices but not restricted to this or any other potential ad- aptation or use." A perfect denouement for a developer: a completely original space that can serve any client.

Computer-generated images in two and three dimensions show how the different elements of the project fit into the shell and relate spatially.

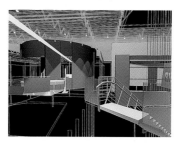 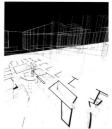

Views of the project during construction.

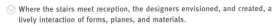

⊗ View of the staircase connecting the two floors. Meeting rooms on each of the office's two levels are visible behind glass at bottom right and top left. Note the parallel vertical wires used to define a plane dividing the stair—and add another visual, textural, and formal tweak to the space.

⊗ Where the stairs meet reception, the designers envisioned, and created, a lively interaction of forms, planes, and materials.

⊗ Offices line both sides of a corridor on the main or upper level. For all its singular, sculpted originality, the office is functional enough to be used by a variety of clients.

⊗ A private meeting room with a dropped ceiling and a custom-designed table.

⊗ The curving gray concrete wall at right encloses the copy room, screening it from reception.

tbwa/chiat/day west coast headquarters

CLIVE WILKINSON ARCHITECTS

Los Angeles, California

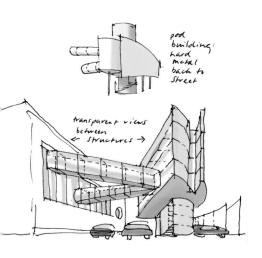

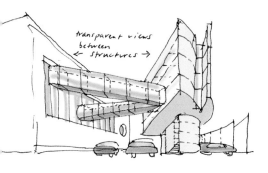

Perhaps more than any other type of enterprise, creative work needs an imaginative environment to succeed in. That's the driving concept behind the headquarters for this advertising agency that requested an open, adaptable office. Clive Wilkinson Architects magically turned an industrial shell into an "advertising city," complete with neighborhoods, green parks, landmark structures, a skyline, and a Main Street.

Basically, the agency wanted to house all 500 employees within a single building—with a little bit of pizzazz. One of the architect's concerns was to keep the company culture integrated, although separated in this 120,000-square-foot (10,800-square-meter) structure. Also guiding the design was the building's 27-foot-high (8.1-meter-high) ceilings. "We decided to create a mezzanine, walkways, and ramps," the architect said, "Getting off the ground was extremely important."

◊ Sketches of the new gatehouse, a metal-clad pavilion connected to the existing warehouse by suspended ramps. The sculptural forms are brightly painted.

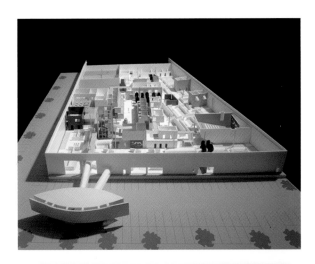

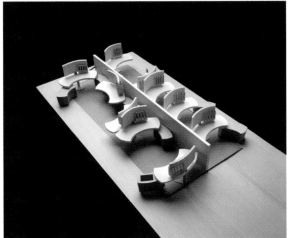

The first step in the design, however, was to bisect the warehouse at its center with Main Street. With a park-like environment with trees, café tables, chairs, and a basketball court at its terminus, Main Street is the central organizing devise. Next, the planning turned to the placement of the creative staff offices. This group, the architect contends, was the hardest to place, as they demanded a degree of privacy as well as centralization. Borrowing from the image of the caves on the Greek Island of Santorini, these offices became "cliff dwellings," brilliant yellow constructions of steel, concrete, and metal decking arranged in two sets of three tiers each flanking Main Street.

⬡ An architectural model shows the internal organization of theTBWA/Chiat/Day offices, an "advertising city" created in a warehouse.

⬡ Model mock-up of workstations.

⬡ View of the "cityscape" from a "cliff dwelling" balcony. The huge screen airs advertising campaigns.

Near the central area is the formal conference room called "Oz," a box made of re-sawn lumber. Adjacent to it is another conference room constructed of three stacked shipping containers. The other "neighborhoods" radiate from this central area and are organized according to agency accounts. For the work stations, Wilkinson developed an adaptable workspace module of metal and wood, called the Nest, that is now being mass produced by Steelcase/Turnstone. These workspaces are interspersed with light tent structures that serve as meeting rooms. One wonders if Clive Wilkinson has studied Carl Gustav Jung, who in 1923 wrote: "The dynamic principle of fantasy is play, which belongs also to the child, and as such it appears to be inconsistent with the principle of serious work. But without this playing with fantasy no creative work has every yet come to birth. The debt we owe to the play of imagination is incalculable." TBWA/Chiat/Day's clients owe something to Clive Wilkinson.

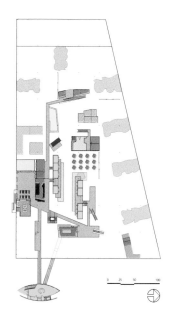

Second floor plan.

First floor plan.

Early sketch of floor plan.

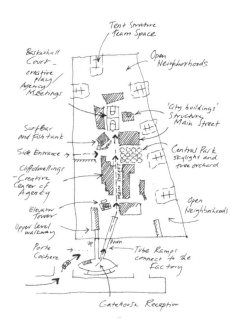

⊘ Early concept drawings of the steel, concrete, and metal decking modules that became known as the "cliff dwellings," and house the creative staff.

Canyon Drive

⊘ A playful rendering of Taco Bell's talking Chihuahua (one of the agency's creation) placed within a cliff dwelling.

⊘ An early concept drawing of the workspace, which was eventually known as the Nest.

rare medium offices

KONING EIZENBERG ARCHITECTURE
Los Angeles, California

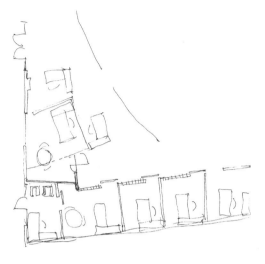

A rough sketch of an early piece of the floor plan, as it was evolving.

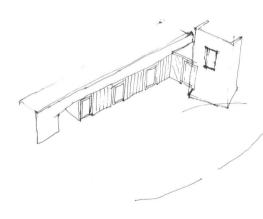

The design of office space for Internet companies presents architects a unique challenge: the clients are accustomed to working in cyberspace and expect things done instantly; the companies turn over frequently, buying and selling one another at a rapid pace; the number of employees can shrink or expand quickly; and the complex technical requirements of the office can shift radically and fast. In general, the owners and operators of these companies demand an image that is fresh, hip, on the edge—and can be changed in six months when the next trend comes along. In other words, everything happens faster; and so the people of the web, inured to this sort of thing, assume that design and architecture happens in the same fashion. Which it normally does not.

The design team from Koning Eizenberg Architecture, headed by Julie Eizenberg, retrofitted 10,700 square feet (963 square meters) of offices for Rare Medium in a small warehouse on the west side of LA. Rare Medium is your basic web business, a multimedia firm that provides Internet sites and web design to a broad range of clients. When the company's owners first approached Koning Eizenberg it had a different name, and e-commerce and web design were just getting off the ground. To gain a sense of how fast things move in that world, you only need to know that this all happened in 1998. Ancient history on the World Wide Web!

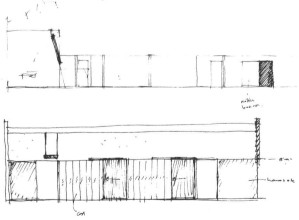

Early drawings show the dynamics of changing materials, levels of transparency and opacity, and wall heights along the perimeter office entrances.

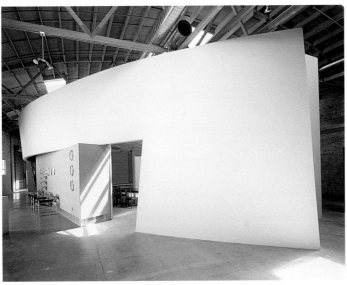

© 1997 Benny Chan-Fotoworks

⊙ The designers inserted a freestanding central container into the middle of the retro-fitted warehouse that serves as Rare Medium's office and studio. Within the tilted, arcing white walls of this structure are various functional spaces: boardroom, copy room, kitchen, server room. The sheetrock walls make a dynamic, counterpoint to the warehouse's existing bowstring truss ceiling system. In this view the reception area lies at left; the boardroom can be seen within the central structure.

⊙ Floor plans with and without written information] show how the designers installed an irregularly shaped, central structure to house the server, workroom, boardroom, kitchen and copy rooms—all much-used, interactive spaces. Offices, workrooms, and other private and semi-private spaces line the perimeter, with open space in between functioning as lounge/gallery zones. The studio at rear is open. Dotted lines indicate mezzanine at far left and top left and top center. The dotted line overlaid on the central structure indicates the location of the high, curving and tilting white walls that enclose it.

The building, complete with a bowstring truss roof system, had been seismically upgraded and emptied out by the landlord. The clients came to Koning Eizenberg "in a hurry and on a tight budget," says Eizenberg, seeking a workplace that projected "contemporary energy and ease." In other words, something cool, hip, and offbeat—all those things that the traditional office is not supposed to be, and trendy web design offices must be. Naturally the offices had to be functional as well, and given the nature of the business, it was imperative that the computer workstations be configured in a manner that was flexible and adaptable. With a bare bones budget of $270,000, the client did not have the funds for new furnishings; so pieces were to be designed and fabricated as budget permitted. Thus the materials are basic: painted sheetrock, MDF plywood, two by fours, and plexiglass. But budget restraints can inspire good work: "The sheetrock is cheap but it also works as a wonderful foil to the wooden ribbed ceiling. There's a great counterpoint of textures," says Eizenberg.

As is evident in plan, the workplace is comprised of a series of small semi-private or open offices and workspaces arranged around the perimeter, with an open studio space and a large, irregularly shaped structure within. This freestanding central structure—actually several

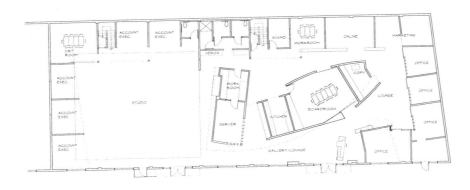

© 1997 Benny Chan-Fotoworks

⊘ At right, offices attain semi-privacy with walls made of
wood structural members and plexiglass panels.

⊘ A view of the central structure from the studio area
at the back of the office. The custom-designed MDF
plywood reception desk is visible at the other end of
the room at right. The server and adjacent workroom
are contained within this end of the central structure. The boxy portal punched through the central
structure at right indicates the space that lies
between the server room and the kitchen.

distinct spaces wrapped within the dynamic embrace of
curving, tilting white sheetrocked walls—remains open
on top, stopping short of the existing bowstring trusses
overhead. Within its walls are various spaces housing
the computers' server, which works as the office hub,
and an adjacent workroom; the company boardroom, finished in MDF grade plywood, and a copy room and a
separate kitchen. The curving, sloping walls of this
white-painted container work as "a great counterpoint"
to the bowstring trusses of the ceiling, and the more rectilinear forms in the space, creating an array of lively
spatial dynamics. As Eizenberg explains it, "When you
have a big box like this, you're trying to fill empty space
with stuff...you use compositional devices (like the tilting white walls) to create a natural flow."

The free areas between the central structure and the
perimeter offices are used as circulation corridors as
well as gallery or lounge space. The perimeter offices are
separated by built-in bookshelves, glass partitions,
and/or drywall and plywood lined walls. In some cases,
wood framing for walls is left without drywall, creating
walls that literally aren't all there. With few private
offices or enclosed rooms, the workplace remains open,
to encourage the collaborative style of work that is nor-
mal for most web-related businesses. The all-important

© 1997 Benny Chan-Fotoworks

⊘ Enclosed yet exposed with wooden structural ribs that echo the ceiling forms, the server
room's banks of computers rest on metal shelving. The open space in foreground is a passage
between the server room and the kitchen. Overhead, a flowing wall creates a partial but continuous enclosure for the central structure.

⊘ A view of the center structure's west end, where the walls meet in a near-collision at the
entrance to the copy room. The new center structure is tucked in beneath the existing bowstring truss ceiling system.

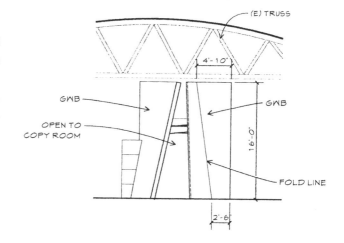

A view of the center structure's west end, where the walls meet in a near-collision at the entrance to the copy room. The new center structure is tucked in beneath the existing bowstring truss ceiling system.

© 1997 Benny Chan-Fotoworks

© 1997 Benny Chan-Fotoworks

data lines that the business requires have been run in oversize conduits and wiring gutters, keeping all the wires accessible for future expansion. A custom-designed plywood reception desk anchors the entrance area. "We try to play with the unexpected," says Eizenberg, "since things change so fast in the dot.com business. In six months things get old. It's like restaurants or retail, where the client is concerned with his image this year. Architecture is becoming more and more like fashion."

Styles change, technologies change, ownership changes. In this environment, you can't really build to last. This project was designed, built, and occupied in under six months. And then, before the architect could complete design of the custom workstation, the company was bought by another. The architect continues to do works for the firm—actually, it was sold again, and a third company—Rare Medium—now owns it. The architect works for a different client, cranking out workstations as fast as they can be fabricated to accommodate Rare Medium's exploding workforce. So it goes, designing three-dimensional workspace for the people creating the digital dimensions of the World Wide Web.

A mezzanine overlooks the boardroom, enclosed by shifting, layered planes of sheetrock and/or homasote panels with plexiglass bases; bookshelves, left, serve a second role, enclosed small offices on the perimeter. The door at left slides shut for privacy when necessary. In the low-tech, low-budget style of web office design, most of the conduit, HVAC, hardware, and other systems hardware are left exposed.

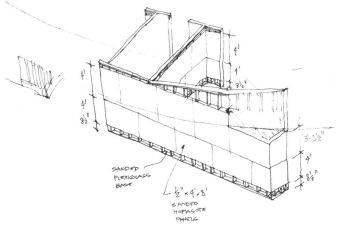

A detailed drawing of the section of the enclosure for the boardroom, constructed of homasote panels with plexiglass bases on a wood frame. The central structure's curving sheet-rock walls here swoop overhead, creating an interesting counterpoint of rectilinearity and curve. The smaller space at left is the kitchen. Detail shows a boxed portal punched into a wall of the central structure.

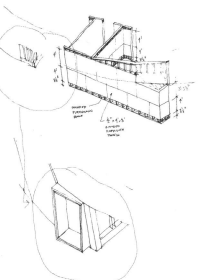

cabana postproduction facility

DAVID LING ARCHITECTS

New York City

○ Architect David Ling cites the great German Expressionist film *The Cabinet of Dr. Caligari* as inspiration for the angular, "shard-like" corridors in the facility.

David Ling's design approach for this facility was "a two-fold aesthetic one, using archaeological editing integrated with modern intervention." A newly merged company devoted to postproduction editing, Cabana required a working environment that combined stylish user-friendly offices for client interaction along with assorted technically sophisticated workspaces. Working with three narrow stories in a Manhattan high rise, Ling linked the levels with an atrium dominated by a monumental stair and a 50-foot-high (15-meter-high) backdrop waterfall. He also employed a common language on all three floors, with folded walls and industrial materials.

Original columns, slabs, and beams were left exposed, with new walls worked in around them. The new walls were "choreographed" according to ideas drawn from music and editing: asymmetric, folded syncopated walls make the melody, while the regularly spaced columns and beams make the rhythm. The irregular facets that compose the walls echo the fragments of film and sound the editors knit together to compose their unified pieces. More specifically, and yet more subtly, the winding, shard-like corridors pay homage to "The Cabinet of Dr. Caligari," the masterpiece of German Expressionist film, while the Odessa steps from Sergei Eisenstein's "Battleship Potemkin" inspired the staircase.

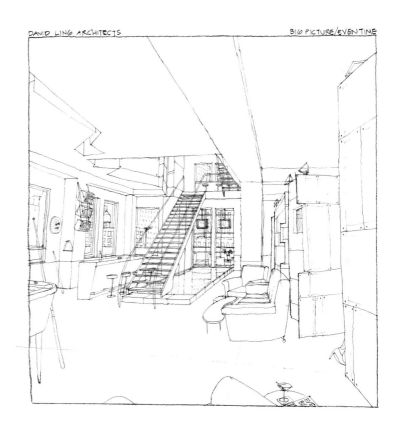

These drawings were done by architect David Ling prior to beginning design, for use in pitching the project to the client. A comparison of drawings and completed project shows that Ling actually took the project in a more radical, distinctive direction once he got going on the design: the stairs in the drawings exhibit none of the sculpted angularity of the finished project. Instead, Ling played up the pleasures of the outdoor terraces—a good selling point for his plan, but unimportant to the real design concept for the building.

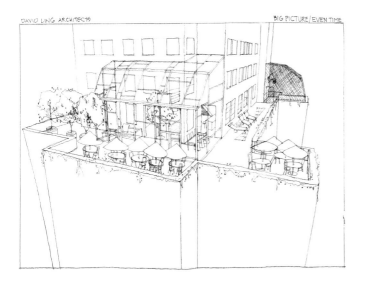

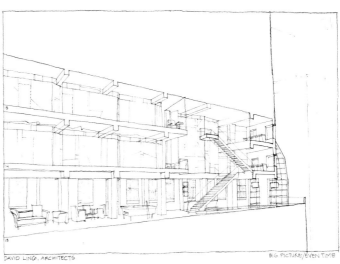

Ling's materials reflect the techy nature of the office, while providing an intriguingly varied palette: walls of backlit corrugated fiberglass, plywood, and galvanized sheet metal form the undulating walls leading from the elevators to the atrium with its backlit fiberglass water-fall, where a thin layer of water flows over the fiberglass and falls into a tear-shaped copper pool. The steel stair-case floats nearby; lit from above and below, it appears to be in the water, or of the water, itself. The atrium's edges are defined by exposed slabs edges, serrated to echo the folding walls; each floor offers a different type of serration, creating a rhythmic dialogue between the floors. Plywood on the opposite wall sets up another rhythm. Natural concrete floors were left unrepaired, then stained with blue and finished with a cracked ice glaze layered atop fragments of old terrazzo, pieces of old marble and brick, and signs of old walls—more archaeology to play off the ductwork, cable trays, sprin-kler pipe, and other functional systems left exposed, playing up the tough industrial nature of the project while also being quite cost effective and permitting easy access for rewiring, a persistent requirement in a facility devoted to postproduction editing work.

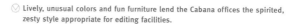
⊘ View illustrates the "dialogue" between materials: concrete, steel, and fiber-glass, and the copper-lined pool at the base of the waterfall.

⊘ Lively, unusual colors and fun furniture lend the Cabana offices the spirited, zesty style appropriate for editing facilities.

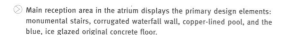
⊘ Main reception area in the atrium displays the primary design elements: monumental stairs, corrugated waterfall wall, copper-lined pool, and the blue, ice glazed original concrete floor.

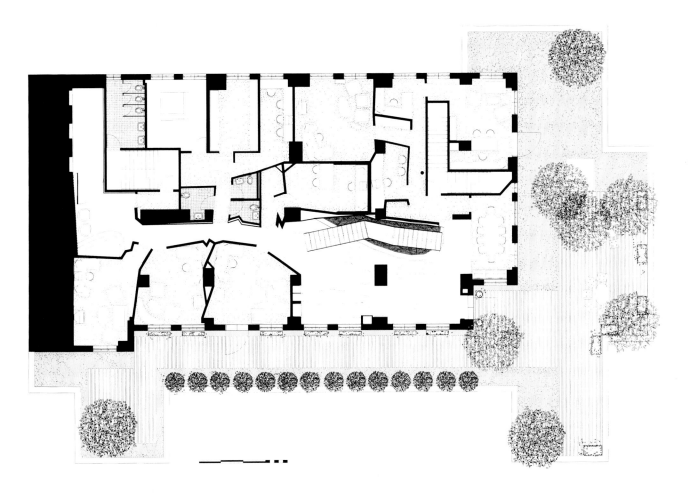

Main entry: floor plan shows the angular corridors at left enclosing offices and meeting space. The sculpted, angular stairs float over the atrium at upper right. The conference room lies at far right. On this level the office also has outdoor terraces on two sides.

The stairs float against the corrugated fiberglass "waterfall."

Images show the dominant element, the staircase, undulating down through the atrium to link the facility's three levels. Architect David Ling claims the Odessa Steps in Eisenstein's "Battleship Potemkin" as inspiration for the stairs.

ten8sixty-five architects' office

STEVEN EHRLICH ARCHITECTS

Culver City, California

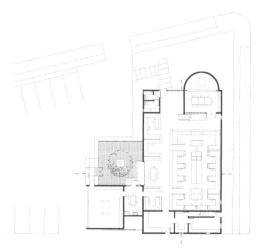

The site plan shows how the building sits on a corner lot.

Rarely has a single building seen such an unusual sequence of functions. The structure now called Ten8Sixty-Five was designed and built in 1917 as the home of the Culver City, California, Municipal Club House, and served as a dance hall and community center. Later, the building found a second life as a mortuary. That use ran its course, and the building had been boarded up and abandoned for years when Steven Ehrlich Architects purchased it for its new firm office.

What Ehrlich describes as a "forensic" visit to the building revealed several positive features that inspired the purchase. When converted from dance hall to funeral parlor, the auditorium had been subdivided into several smaller rooms with hung ceilings, including a semi-circular viewing room at the front of the building. In exploring the attic that existed over these various rooms, the architect discovered a long-span wood truss roof system. Beneath various layers of flooring and grungy carpets, was a maple floor—the dance floor of old.

The architect's early sketches show the fundamental plan, at top left, and a view of the building, bottom left. At top right, a rough section; at bottom right, a more detailed rough plan that is pretty much true to the plan as built.

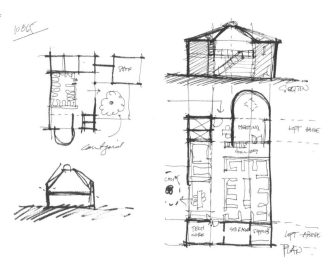

The former dance hall turned mortuary turned architects' office called Ten8Sixty-Five (10865 is the building's street number) presents a unique façade to the street, with the semi-circular former mortuary viewing room now transformed into a conference room by the architect. The thin sash windows recall designs from the early twentieth century, when the structure was built.

And so the challenge became, notes Ehrlich, "to honor the spirit of the building (and its previous occupants) yet not be a slave to its preservation." The architect sought to create a lively, light-filled office, saving what could be salvaged. To this end the structure was stripped down to its essential shell. The façade was demolished, but neither the footprint nor the principal rooflines changed. An open "atelier" style office was created in keeping with the culture of the practice. Long spans required for the library on the mezzanine level and the conference room on the ground floor led to the insertion of steel moment frames. Aluminum sash in a "thin line" detail recalls steel windows of the early twentieth century.

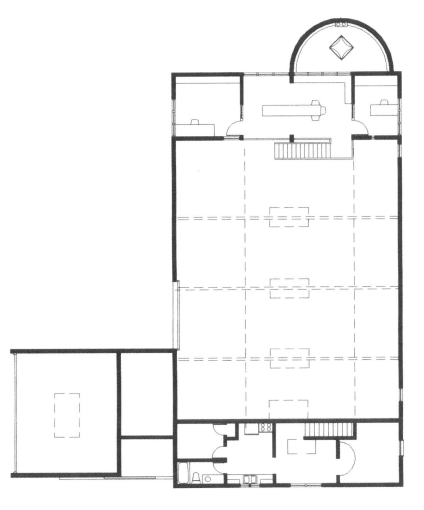

Architectural models and minimal furnishings distinguish the gallery/waiting area; the stairs thrusting into the area lead up to the mezzanine.

An eighty-five-year-old rubber tree on the site became the focal point of an outdoor courtyard defined by a plastic and wood-framed wall. A 14-foot-square glass roll-up garage door dissolves the barrier between inside and outside, and floods the interior with daylight and fresh air. A fixed perimeter wall of clear-finished MDF defines the work zone; aluminum accents unify coffee and conference tabletops, bathroom counters, credenzas, and workstations. The workstations are constructed of Finland color birch plywood partitions with linoleum tops on solid doors.

As Ehrlich notes, as "a model of adaptive re-use the offices simultaneously embrace both the spiritual and environmental issues of recycling. On the material plane the rejuvenation of a discarded structure conserves building materials and requires less energy to light, heat, and cool. At the same time, human dedication to a dynamic future converges with the past in the architects' conference room, formerly the mortuary's viewing room."

Before the architects opened the doors of their new atelier, a sage-burning ceremony was conducted and holy water blessed by a local priest. All souls who might be lingering from days past were invited to attend.

An eighty-five-year old rubber tree dominates the courtyard, defined by a wood and plastic wall, and entered through a portal crowned with a lively, angular canopy. When the glass roll-up door separating the courtyard from the adjacent interior conference room is rolled up, inside and outside become one.

⊗ Seen from ground-level and from various points along the mezzanine loft in the front of the
⊘ building, the central open work area is contained within a wall of clear-finish MDF. Workstations are made of birch plywood partitions with linoleum desktops on solid wood doors. One
reason the architect purchased the building was the discovery, in attics above hung ceilings
(later removed), of the original wood truss roofing system, still intact.

⊘ The conference room in the front right of the building, seen from within and from the gallery
inside the entry on the main floor; a second conference area lies in the mezzanine level library,
above.

the pearl district office
of mahlum architects

DESIGN BY ANNE SCHOPF, MICHAEL SMITH, AND MILES WOOFTER, MAHLUM ARCHITECTS

INDUSTRIAL DESIGN BY JACK KEARNEY, COMPANY K

Portland, Oregon

The Pearl District near downtown is Portland's answer to SoHo: Vintage concrete and masonry buildings, formerly used for light manufacturing, now attract the city's creative types ranging from artists to ad agencies to dot-com entrepreneurs. And architects, too, are drawn to the buzz, the street-level liveliness, and especially the high-ceilinged, loft-style interiors. Mahlum's search for Pearl District space ended on the ground floor at the Prael Hegele building, a brick edifice from 1906 originally built for a crockery and glass wholesaler. Great street presence and easy access more than made up for the somewhat awkward shape of the 4,840-square foot available space, which snakes between and around other tenants in a kind of choppy T-shape. Anne Schopf took the lead in configuring the space to best serve the firm's needs while utilizing the existing grid of the heavy timber warehouse structure.

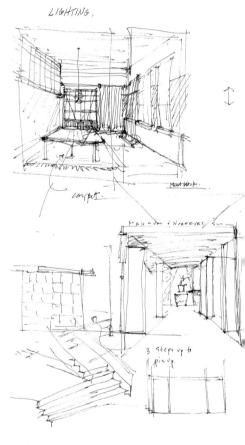

Pages from architect Schopf's notebook reveal early concepts of the space, including rough floorplans, lighting ideas, and sketches of hardware and other components. Schopf often uses words—conceptual language—as a means of generating design ideas.

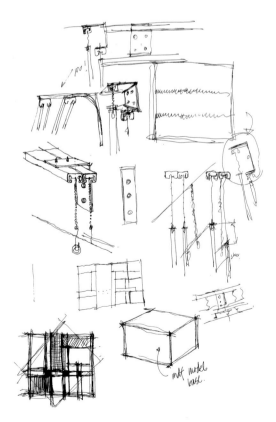

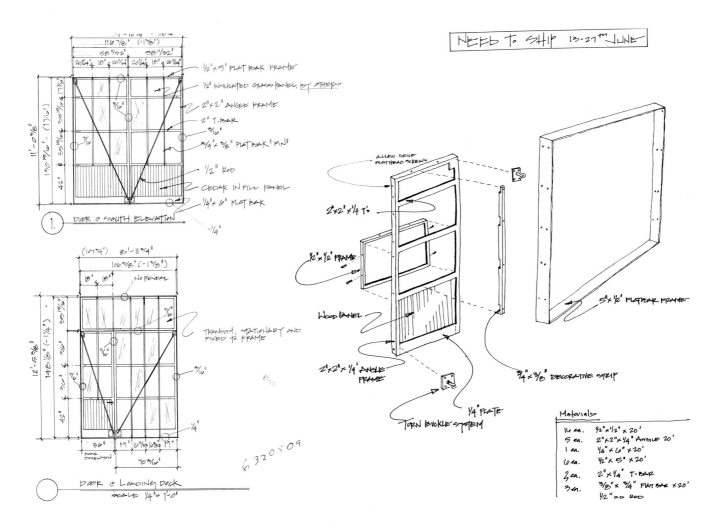

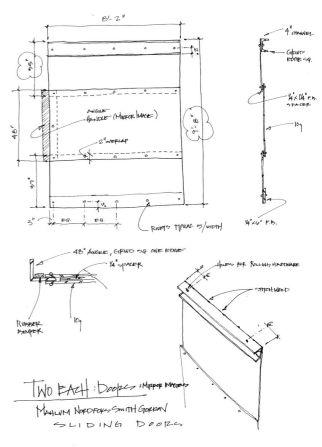

⬠ Kearney's drawings reflect his more detail-oriented task: he not only designs the hardware, doors, floors, and other components, but also oversees assembly. Kearney does not use a computer, as is evident in these simple but detailed drawings for the two entry doors at the Mahlum office.

◌ Drawings detail overview and components of riveted plate steel conference and presentation room doors with industrial strength hardware. They can be rolled closed for privacy.

▽ Drawings detail the turnbuckle systems for the entry doors on the old loading dock. On plan, they are located at bottom, just right of center.

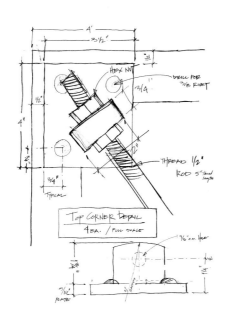

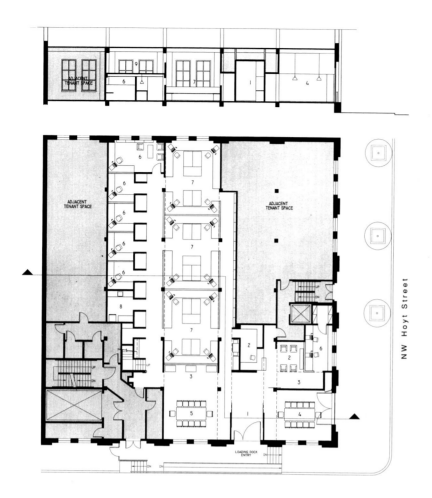

⊗ Floorplan of irregularly shaped ground-floor space, with conference, reception, and other more "public" areas at bottom right, and the long design studio and private offices occupying the 100-foot-long volume that stretches from one end of the building to the other. The windows at top were punched out during the renovation of the space. The main entry at bottom is off an old loading dock.

⊗ A view into the conference room seen from street level. Original doors were replaced with pivoting steel and glass doors that can be opened in mild weather.

⊗ View through the entry lobby, with sliding steel doors closed on flanking conference and presentation rooms. The transition from the loading dock to office reflects the project's historical and contextual honesty, with cast iron, riveted steel plate doors, industrial lighting fixtures, and steel flooring.

The office is organized around a 20 foot wide (6 meters wide), 100-foot-long (30.5 meters long) east-west volume that serves as the design studio as well as organizing element and circulation spine. With a bank of new windows punched out at the east end to "create an equalized container of elongated proportions," notes Schopf, the studio contains both open workstation areas and private offices. The design "focuses on the nature of how we work in teams" according to Schopf, "and on the nature and spirit of the original warehouse." Accessed via a front door located on a former loading dock, the reception area, conference and presentation rooms, and gallery space, devoted to showing the work of emerging artists, all face the street to the west and south. They flow into the open design studio to the east, thus establishing what Schopf describes as "a design that layers from the most public spaces (lobby, conference rooms, reception and gallery) to the most private offices." Schopf also sought to create a design that played with contrasts and ambiguities: "hard and soft, light and dark, expansive and intimate" are three of the paired qualities the design evokes through the orchestration of space and form, and especially the use of materials.

View of the conference room from the reception lobby. Schopf specified 14 foot (4 meter) velvet curtains to create a softening counterpoint to all the hard surfaces and textures. The conference room occupies the most prominently "public" corner of the building, on the southwest.

After some trial and error Kearney created leather pulls for the riveted plate steel doors, hung on industrial hardware, that roll closed for conference room privacy.

Detail of curtains and two types of flooring illustrate the subtle textural and color changes employed to provide richness: maple, sisal, and velvet make a quietly provocative mix.

Seeking to specify a materials palette that "reflects the history of the neighborhood," Schopf turned to Kearney to give form to her vision. "She comes to me and tells me what she wants or needs," he says "then I design it, she reacts to it, and we hammer it out." In the Pearl District office project, Kearney's major contributions included several different types of steel doors, entry area floors made of salvaged steel plates, and a reception desk sculpted from re-used leather belts from the papermaking industry, laminated hardboard countertops, and steel. His designs for these components reflect a scrupulous attention to detail and a profound knowledge of the materials—and they're specified to work in concert with the existing concrete, wood floors, heavy timbers, and other original elements. As Schopf puts it, "It was a taking of the industrial elements and materials and transforming them through detailing and finish; taking that which was originally rough and honoring it through careful treatment."

Separating Anne Schopf's architecture from Jack Kearney's industrial design can be a tricky business, not unlike trying to parse a similar line of demarcation in their relationship—one that separates the personal from the professional. The couple have been friends since childhood in western New York, married for the last five years, and have collaborated on a number of projects in the Pacific Northwest, most notably the office/studios in Portland, Oregon, and Seattle, Washington, for Mahlum Architects. Schopf has worked at Mahlum for the past decade, while Kearney in 1998 left a well-known Seattle industrial design firm to open his own studio, Company K. Recently promoted to principal at Mahlum, Schopf has given this relatively conservative firm a sharper, more challenging design edge in the last few years, particularly on collaborative projects with Kearney like Mahlum's Portland office.

Professional relations can strain personal relationships, but Kearney and Schopf seem to have achieved a successful modus operandi: they describe their collaborations as "a confrontational process, because we both have strong ideas and high expectations. We don't mince words." For example, Schopf describes Kearney's first version of the leather door pulls in the Mahlum office as "looking like sanitary napkins." Needless to say, Kearney redesigned. High expectations imply great respect for each other's talents, and that respect is well-earned, judging by this project and others they collaborated on under the aegis of Mahlum, including the Doc Martens Airwair Offices, and Mahlum's recently completed Seattle offices.

300 california street
light box wall

HUNTSMAN ARCHITECTURAL GROUP

San Francisco, California

Originally constructed in the 1940s and remodeled in the 1980s, 300 California Street, a renovation project in the heart of San Francisco's financial district, represents a fine example of architecture employed as a marketing tool. When the building's owners hired Huntsman Architectural Group to do another remodel, they had more than a facelift in mind: they sought to reposition 300 California as a facility for "new economy" tenants. New economy means dot-coms, media companies, and others in the high tech sector—the kind of companies that have transformed San Francisco's SoMa, or "South of Market" neighborhood into a vibrant new work-and-play destination. Huntsman's challenge was to create something unique—a "South of Market"-style building in the heart of the relatively staid north of Market financial district.

Working with the building owners, the architect elected to focus its efforts on key areas of the building rather than attempt to reconfigure the entire exterior. Instead, the designers created a dramatic focal point with a new entrance and street-level lobby.

The designers floated a red ceiling panel within the new, expanded lobby area as a dynamic element contrasting with original concrete columns, walls, and ceilings, and new aluminum panels and fixtures.

First, they demolished the existing lobby, replacing it with a larger, more prominent volume. On the exterior façade, they created a composition of stainless steel panels along with an oversized, steel-framed window capped by overlapping metal brows.

Now highly visible from the street, the lobby interior dramatically contrasts raw, natural materials such as board-formed poured concrete and steel panels with refined, tectonic elements including extruded aluminum and glass. The most striking visual feature in the new lobby, a cubist-inspired wall of aluminum-framed, illuminated glass, was custom-designed, but constructed from stock materials. Existing concrete columns, walls, and ceilings were exposed, the rawness of these materials enhancing the newly defined low-tech/high-tech character of the building. A ceiling panel in bright red adds a colorful, dynamic element, while a sleekly polished black terrazzo floor pulls it all together, helping to establish the building as a stylish, SoMa-influenced outpost in the financial district.

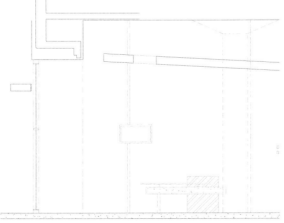

Elevation shows the lobby with built-in reception desk and floating ceiling hung at a slight angle.

Stainless steel panels and brows, and expanses of glass, lend the new lobby a strong street presence, enriched with a red ceiling and an illuminated glass and aluminum feature wall. The lobby's dynamic, energetic quality comes from the contrast of raw, natural finishes and sleek materials. The black terrazzo floor serves as a grounding element, uniting new and old.

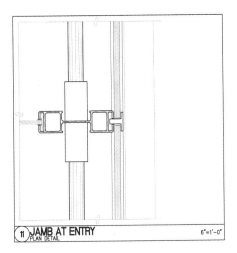

11 **JAMB AT ENTRY** PLAN DETAIL 6"=1'-0"

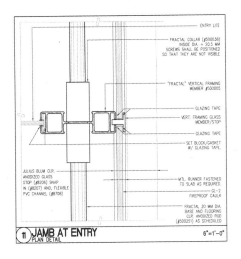

ENTRY LITE

FRACTAL COLLAR (#500038)
INSIDE DIA. = 20.5 MM
SCREWS SHALL BE POSITIONED
SO THAT THEY ARE NOT VISIBLE

"FRACTAL" VERTICAL FRAMING
MEMBER #500005

GLAZING TAPE

VERT. FRAMING GLASS
MEMBER/STOP

GLAZING TAPE

SET BLOCK/GASKET
W/ GLAZING TAPE.

JULIUS BLUM CLR.
ANODIZED GLASS
STOP (#8206) SNAP
IN (#8207) AND, FLEXIBLE
PVC CHANNEL (#8708)

MTL. RUNNER FASTENED
TO SLAB AS REQUIRED.

GL-2
FIREPROOF CAULK

FRACTAL 20 MM DIA.
BASE AND FLOORING
CLR. ANODIZED ROD
(#500251) AS SCHEDULED

11 **JAMB AT ENTRY** PLAN DETAIL 6"=1'-0"

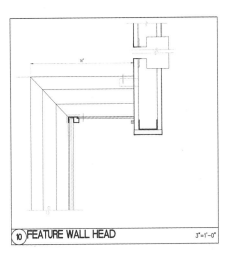

14"

10 **FEATURE WALL HEAD** 3"=1'-0"

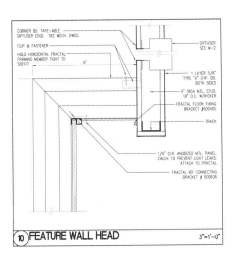

CORNER BD. TAPE-ABLE
DIFFUSER EDGE. SEE MECH. DWGS.

CLIP & FASTENER

HOLD HORIZONTAL FRACTAL
FRAMING MEMBER TIGHT TO
SOFFIT

14"

DIFFUSER
SEE M-2

1 LAYER 5/8"
TYPE "X" GYP. BD.
BOTH SIDES

4" 18GA MTL. STUD,
18" O.C. W/KICKER

FRACTAL FLOOR FIXING
BRACKET #500405

TRACK

1/4" CLR. ANODIZED MTL. PANEL.
CAULK TO PREVENT LIGHT LEAKS.
ATTACH TO FRACTAL

FRACTAL 90° CONNECTING
BRACKET # 500606

10 **FEATURE WALL HEAD** 3"=1'-0"

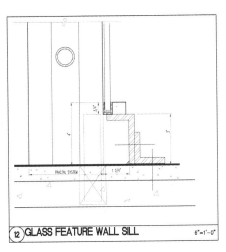

FRACTAL SYSTEM 1 3/4"

12 **GLASS FEATURE WALL SILL** 6"=1'-0"

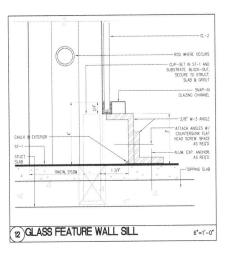

GL-2

ROD WHERE OCCURS

CLIP-SET IN ST-1 AND
SUBSTRATE. BLOCK-OUT,
SECURE TO STRUCT.
SLAB & GROUT

SNAP-IN
GLAZING CHANNEL

3/8" M-3 ANGLE

ATTACH ANGLES W/
COUNTERSUNK FLAT
HEAD SCREW. SPACE
AS REQ'D.

ALUM. EXP. ANCHOR,
AS REQ'D.

CAULK @ EXTERIOR

ST-1

STUCT.
SLAB

FRACTAL SYSTEM 1 3/4"

TOPPING SLAB

12 **GLASS FEATURE WALL SILL** 6"=1'-0"

CAD-generated drawings, show construction details of the door jamb and feature wall, newly designed elements in the lobby.

doc martens airwair USA headquarters offices

DESIGN BY ANNE SCHOPF, MICHAEL SMITH, PHIL CHUBB, MAHLUM ARCHITECTS
INDUSTRIAL DESIGN BY JACK KEARNEY

Portland, Oregon

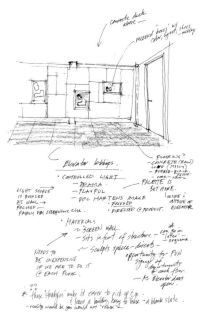

Schopf translates her written ideas into visual images, with further notes about details, colors, and other specifics.

Since early in the twentieth century Doc Martens prospered as a successful manufacturer of shoes and boots for heavy duty work. That is, until the 1970s, when big, clunky, and practical Doc Martens leather boots were discovered by punk rockers and their punk followers, and thus became trendy, sending the company into a different realm of marketing and style. Through subsequent generations of rock n' rollers, the industrial strength stompers have remained hip, and many a tattooed, lip-pierced wannabe punk rocker wouldn't dream of stepping outside without first strapping on his or her Doc Martens. And so when the Portland, Oregon-based company went looking for a new headquarters building, it headed first to the trendy Pearl District, the city's burgeoning art-and-design neighborhood, home to galleries, ad agencies, web designers, cool boutiques—and Mahlum Architects, whose own street level Pearl District office, designed by firm architect Anne Schopf and industrial designer (and Schopf's husband and lifelong friend) Jack Kearney, served notice that Mahlum Architects had a fix on the post-industrial chic of the neighborhood aesthetic. Doc Martens' planners certainly took note, commissioning Mahlum to plan their move to a new headquarters.

Computer-generated images helped the architect explain in advance how the project would look after completion.

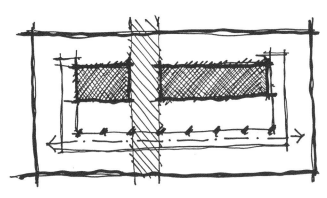

Rough sketch of floor plan illustrates how architect Schopf envisioned the single circulation corridor positioned between the oversize core and the workstations along the window walls.

Floor plans of ground level show the deployment of open plan workstations along window walls and private offices on window corners or on the interior side of the circulation corridor, adjacent to the core. The grid of columns at 10-foot (3-meter) intervals determined the layout of the space.

Image of typical floor prior to renovation shows the columns at 10-foot (3-meter) intervals that in large measure determined the layout.

The Airwair people were in a hurry to move, however. Rushed for time, the company ended up buying a problematic structure—a six-story concrete building from the early 1900s, originally built as an SRO residential hotel, with only 9 foot, 6 inch floor to floor (not floor to ceiling) height (2.85 meter), and 10 foot (3 meter) spacing between columns. In other words, though located on the edge of the loft district, the space was far from lofty, an irony especially hard to take for Doc Martens' top executives: the company's CEO and COO are each nearly 7 feet (2.1 meters) tall. According to Schopf, "the building was bland, and kind of a nightmare, with a depressingly monotonous floor plate; the challenge was to make the 3,500-square-foot (315-square-meter) floors feel spacious yet efficient, dynamic, and most importantly, industrial," in keeping with the style of the neighborhood.

Schopf's design developed through a series of brainstorming sessions and then solitary note taking and drawings. As it evolved the plan entailed organizing the floors by departments—Finance & Credit, Customer Service, Marketing, Sales & Showroom—then placing conference and lounge space on top. Schopf designed each floor with the same essential layout, then added variations. She incorporated the existing and unmovable concrete columns as the primary element of organization and circulation, revolving around a large central core containing elevator and stairs. With the oversized core allowing room for only a single double-loaded corridor on each floor, the design team located the open office workstations, designed by Schopf and Kearney, on the window walls to access views. The private offices were situated on the interior behind sliding translucent doors to enhance light flow, with dividing walls stopping short of the ceiling to expand the sense of space. Kearney's custom-designed pivoting doors access corner offices; alternating with the custom sliders along the circulation corridors, the doors stretch to the ceiling to create a vertical element.

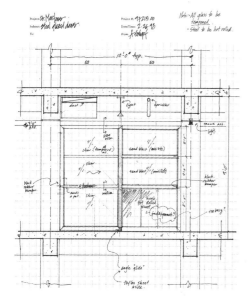

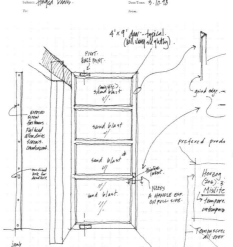

○ By the time Schopf's drawings get to industrial designer Kearney and the project fabricators, they have attained a high level of detail. The doors vary in height and hardware, with the corner office doors on pivots and the corridor office doors on sliders.

○ Industrial designer Kearney's two drawings illustrate the structural specifics for assembling the reception desk, designed by Kearney and architect Schopf.

Schopf and Kearney's contextual evocation of industrial ambience was initiated by stripping the building to its shell. The concrete columns and ceilings were sandblasted and sealed, leaving exposed century-old aggregate of river rock and brick. In a serendipitous turn of events, the rich patina of these existing elements became a major element in the overall composition. To further the industrial look the designers left exposed conduit, sprinkler lines, and mechanical ducts, with all connections and transitions carefully detailed. Under the design direction of Kearney, hot rolled steel was fabricated into doors, light fixtures, and the reception desk, with visible welds and hardware specified to emphasize the gritty, workaday aspect of the building. As Kearney bluntly puts it, "We had to make a lot of stuff, and we were working with a low budget. Steel is cheap." VG fir was introduced into the workstations and reception desk to contrast with the hard, cool palette, and because "I like the mix of steel and wood," notes Kearney. Schopf specified carpeting for sound control in the low-ceilinged, hard-surfaced work areas, with cork flooring employed to delineate circulation paths.

○ The designers enclosed custom-designed workstations with simple planes of VG fir, and sealed the original columns but otherwise left them untouched.

○ Architect Schopf collaborated with industrial designer Jack Kearney on design of the steel and sandblasted doors that enclose the corner offices on recessed pivot hinges.

◇ A view of the main lobby, with a mural of the original Doc Martens' 1460 model painted on the back wall. The steel and fir reception desk dominates the room and was designed to evoke the look of the product. Steel and wood make a great, low-cost combination.

◇ Two views of private offices along main and side corridors. The offices are enclosed by custom-designed, translucent sliding glass doors that stop short of the ceiling. Note the fusion of original aggregate concrete with exposed conduit, ductwork, sprinkler pipes, and other elements including a cork floor. The corner office at the end of the hall features a pivot door that reaches to the ceiling to bring in a little verticality, and for the sake of variation.

learn it! stair/entry

HUNTSMAN ARCHITECTURAL GROUP

San Francisco, California

⊘ Hovering over the stairs, layered sheet metal panels scale down the 20-foot-high (6 meter-high) space. The materials—plastic, metal, and concrete—signal the raw but sleek industrial look of the contemporary high-tech office.

The designers from the Huntsman Architectural Group call the Learn It! project a "stair as entry sign." In the context of client and site, it's an apt description.

The client, Learn It!, is a computer training company. For the basement level offices, the architect had developed a high-tech look, with metal finishes, open ceilings, and industrial accents—the raw but sleek look of the contemporary dot-com office. At the same time, the building owners approached the Huntsman designers to explore the feasibility of building a second exit to permit build-out of the basement level. After the designers had completed several studies, a street-level tenant left the building. At that time the clients and designers together agreed that putting a small amount of street-level space into play as a primary entry stair would significantly increase the value of the basement level, resulting in a higher overall rent.

The challenge, then, was to create a grand staircase that would reflect the same high-tech aesthetic as the basement level offices. This stair was to have visual appeal at street level—to work as a sign. The main problem was one of scale, for the basements have 8-foot (2.4-meter) ceilings, while the entry soars up to a height of 20 feet (6 meters).

The client and designers collaboratively elected to create a staircase that would not read as solid but would instead appear transparent, a "floating form that would draw visitors inside." The look is industrial modern, with a sense of humor meant to appeal to the young. Notes project designer Tim Murphy, "Our inspiration was patio furniture. We liked plastic, sparkle, and metal."

Sheet metal layers hover over the stairs, cloud-like, reducing the 20-foot (6-meter) scale. A sandwich of two types of plastic sheeting encloses the staircase, lending it a lantern-like glow. Distinctive circular pendant lamps float overhead, glowing like little planets. Treads and risers are constructed of subway grating. The look is high tech, industrial, sleek but edgy enough to signal the fresh, youth-oriented Learn It! Style.

Signage, light fixtures, and especially the artful interplay of horizontal and vertical elements, aglow behind big windows, lend the entry and staircase a strong visual appeal on the street level.

The stairs' treads and risers are made of subway grating.

The panels enclosed the staircase are made of two types of plastic sheeting sandwiched together. Note the slightly skewed vertical supports.

Computer-generated drawing show stair from two perspectives, with plastic sheeting, light fixtures, and horizontal floating panels.

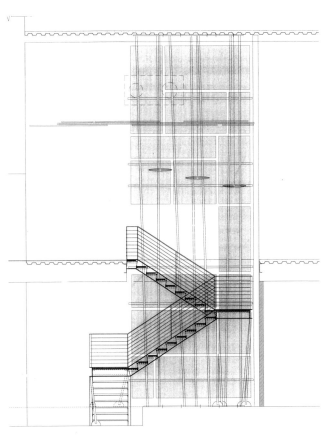

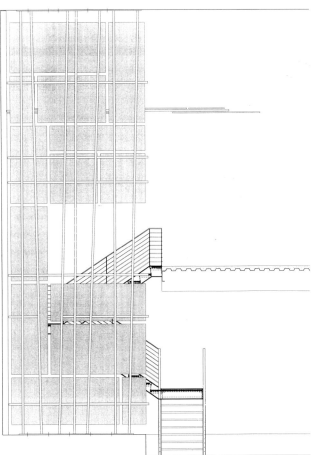

my garage studio & office

GGLO ARCHITECTS

Denver, Colorado

Located in an historic Denver neighborhood, My Garage is a three-bay masonry brick structure built in 1923, with concrete floors, steel windows, and an open, curved ceiling supported by steel bowstring trusses. In renovating and remodeling the structure, at the client's request the designers recycled many of these forms, even reusing original concrete, roof decking and other materials as part of an effort to make the building as "green" as possible.

In My Garage, a design team including artist Misty Todd and architects Clayton O'Brien Smith and Don Mackay (both from the Seattle firm GGLO) transformed an old auto repair shop into a lively art gallery and office space for a Denver oil magnate. In doing so they also made a home for Bambi, the oilman's vintage airstream trailer, a classic that he'd kept at various rig sites in the early years of his career. Bambi the Trailer, several curving walls made from parts of old oil tanks, and other oil business artifacts and souvenirs look perfectly at home here, mingling with an eclectic but serious collection of modern art. Additionally, the project's new kitchen and bathroom display the same quirky high style that infuses both the gallery and office zones. The interior subdivision, accomplished with an assortment of freestanding walls and angular, off-center structures, breaks the space down into offices, gallery, kitchen, bath, reception, and other storage and utility areas. The largest volume, in the central bay, is left completely open—Bambi occupies prime real estate along one side—and given over to gallery display space, with the offices and other functional zones located in the flanking bays.

A view across the gallery space, where a pair of modern works occupy two walls flanking a passage that leads to the main office area. At rear, a section of an old oil tank helps screen the office area. Above, original bowstring steel trusses were saved, with new openable skylights installed to aid in air circulation as well as enhance the artificial lighting with daylight.

Built in 1923 in what has become a historically significant Denver neighborhood, My Garage now houses an art gallery and office space behind these original masonry and glass paned walls. Select panes have been left clear for viewing; the rest are sandblasted to maintain privacy.

◎ The owner's vintage airstream trailer, nicknamed Bambi, occupies a place of honor on the edge of the open gallery space in the midst of the project.

Energy conservation and creation was promoted as well, by use of 25 percent more roof insulation and 35 percent more wall insulation than required; new and recycled skylights feature UV heat mirror glazing to minimize lighting loads; openable windows and skylights provide flow-through ventilation in lieu of air conditioning; gas fired hot water heating and ventilation was installed, and zoned for separate spaces to minimize waste; low-wattage lamps and lighting controls were also used. In the exterior landscape, low water plantings were selected, the lawn was minimized, and a low water irrigation system installed.

◎ Comfortable, stylish modern furnishings and a new wood floor lend an upscale but relaxed tone to the oilman's office located in one of the end bays of the garage. Visible at right, a section of an old oil tank provides a privacy screen.

◎ A two-tiered, steel-topped desk greets visitors at the reception area. All the major walls in the interior have been used to hang pieces from the owner's extensive collection of modern art.

In developing the plan for the building, the architect went back and forth with the client in an intense effort at reaching a clear understanding of the goal, as is evident in the documents and drawings shown here. They covered everything from the way the three bays should function individually to the number of window panes that should be left clear or sandblasted. The photographs offers evidence that the process worked: with Bambi the Trailer holding center stage, My Garage offers a generously-scaled, eccentrically amusing theater for work, art, and play, demonstrating that the boundaries between these activities and forms of expression can and should remain open wherever and whenever possible.

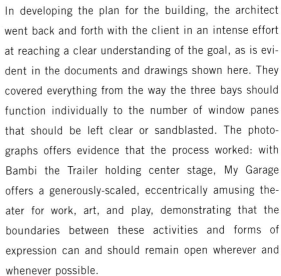

◎ A view from one end of the "oil tank wall" back through the passage and across the gallery to the trailer. The interaction of angled and curving walls as well as different colors, textures, materials, and eccentric art works creates a lively visual dynamic in the space.

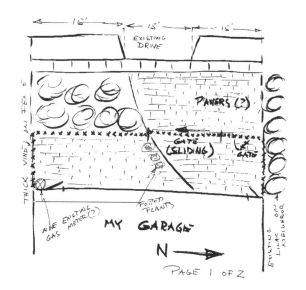

The rusting interior side of an old oil tank serves as a screen or wall, and bears comparison with minimalist sculpture. The delicate flowers atop their industrial strength pedestals made a nice contrast.

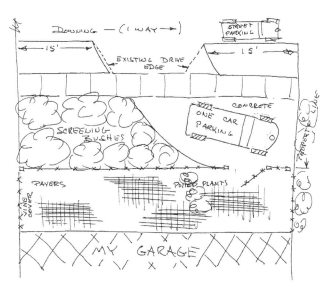

Two days of faxes with notes and drawings from the client to the architect with thoughts on how the landscaping in front of the building should work.

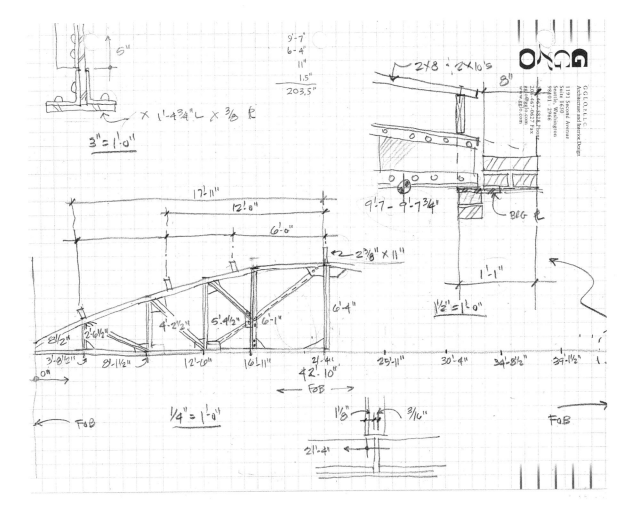

○ Architect's measurements and drawings on the existing steel bowstring truss system.

○ Two drawings with the architect's ideas for the glass panes on the façade, and the client's response which eliminates some of the clear, see-through panes in for greater privacy and light control.

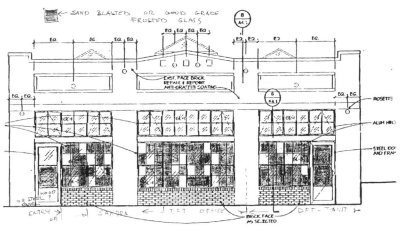

8%. ■, I HAVE LOCATED THEM THINKING OF SANDRA'S AREA, MY DESK, MY EASY CHAIR & MY PAINT AREA. THE TWO IN THE UPPER TIER ARE ONLY FOR EFFECT EXCEPT AS WE SUBSTANTIALLY ALTER THE FRONT LAYOUT (OR AS MISTY OR YOU DON'T AGREE) THIS WILL BE IT.

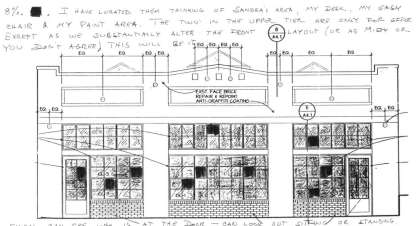

- SANDRA CAN SEE WHO IS AT THE DOOR - CAN LOOK OUT SITTING OR STANDING.
- I CAN DO THE SAME FROM MY DESK AS WELL AS WHERE THE AMES CHAIR IS PROBABLY GOING TO BE

the children's place
corporate headquarters

DAVIS BRODY BOND

Secaucus, New Jersey

⊘ Ground floor plan shows store mock-up areas in lower right hand corner and team area in upper right.

⊘ Workspaces in the team area were designed to be flexible to encourage cross communication.

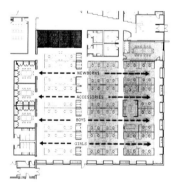

For the rehabilitation of its headquarters, design became a means to facilitate communication between the traditionally separate departments of this corporation. In fact, that ease of collaboration and communication was the key driver behind the interior design and space planning of The Children's Place Corporate Headquarters by Davis Brody Bond. The solution was a highly adaptable, flexible space through which the conception, development, and marketing of a specific product can be carefully—and successfully-tracked.

Davis Brody Bond started with an office/warehouse complex in Secaucus, New Jersey, 10 miles from midtown Manhattan, where the company was located. By expanding the upper level in the high bay, the warehouse could be rehabilitated to accommodate at least 350 people, enough to meet the corporation's needs well into 2001.

A fast growing retailer of apparel and accessories for boys, girls and newborns, The Children's Place merchandising strategy centers on the marketing of a collection of interchangeable outfits and accessories to create a distinctive coordinated look. The corporate leaders, therefore, desired a workspace that allowed close collaboration and interaction between all of their workers—designers, production, retailers, and marketers—and across product lines. The boys' department should have first hand knowledge of what the girls department was producing and so forth.

The most significant space of the entire 70,000-square-foot (6,300-square-meters) structure in relationship to the workings of the corporation is the "multiple team area." Here in a series of different styles of workspaces are located the design teams of each project line. Directly adjacent to them are the workspaces of the merchandising area teams. Next come the workspaces of the product development teams and then the project team rooms. The merchandise executive offices are off to one side. This arrangement facilitates cross-pollination between designers and departments.

In the design, Davis Brody Bond worked closely with DEGW, a specialist consultant in programming and planning the workplace. DEGW examined the benefits to be gained from different workplace space designs, which it identified as the den, clue, hive, and cell. The architects based the space requirements on extensive interviews, surveys, and workshop, and elaborate modeling.

The headquarters also contains a full-scale mock-up of a typical retail store, which is used to develop display and merchandising strategies for each product line and the company's distribution center.

⊗ Top: A photo montage of perspective clients lines one wall of the employee cafeteria.

⊗ A skylight brings natural daylight into the cafeteria.

A metal stair leads to the second story extension of the cafeteria.

The employee cafeteria extends to a second, skylit level.

Employees are given the opportunity to relax in a small lounge area beneath the stairs in the cafeteria.

⊗ The design offers small nooks for more private contemplation.

⊗ The boardroom provides built-in, high-tech amenities.

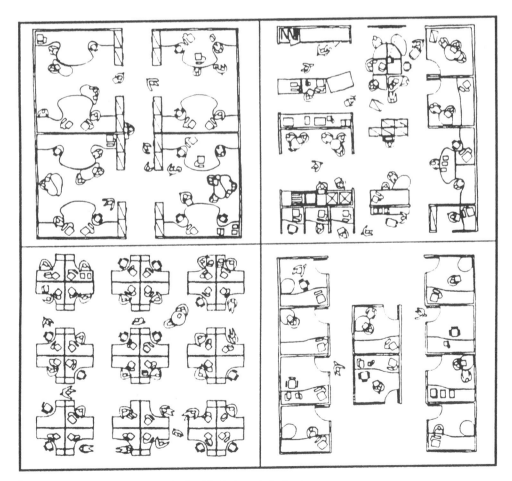

⊗ Pages from the Strategic Design Program developed for the Corporate Headquarters for the Children's Design Place illustrate the different workplace designs known as the Den.

crabtree & evelyn store

KUWABARA PAINE MCKENNA BLUMBERG (KPMB) ARCHITECTS

King of Prussia, Pennsylvania

Located in a mall in King of Prussia, Pennsylvania, the Crabtree & Evelyn store shown here was designed as a prototype for a series of stores located across the country. In this mall location, a floor-to-ceiling glass storefront enhances street presence and visibility. The natural qualities of the products are underscored by the organic, leafy forms of display tables, niches, and cabinets.

Models for the prototype store in King of Prussia, Pennsylvania. This store had a 2,400-square-foot (216-square-meter) floor plan and a floor-to-ceiling glass storefront. The two large vertical elements in the foreground frame the entry. As is evident in the large number of components on the "floor," the designers offered myriad variations on the designs of the floating display elements.

With stores located in various sized facilities throughout the United States, the Crabtree & Evelyn company foresaw the need for a flexible design prototype to be the basis for a new generation of its retail outlets that appeal to a younger, more sophisticated clientele. The Canadian firm of KPMB developed three different sized stores as architectural models as a "kit of parts" for Crabtree and Evelyn to choose alternative store designs. The first prototype store is located in Richmond, Virginia.

Purveyors of high-end soaps, lotions, and other hygiene and health-related products, Crabtree & Evelyn knew exactly what they wanted in each section of the store, with specific areas designated for soaps, bath toiletries, aromatherapy products, food products, home accessories, and gardening products. The models proved to be very successful, providing immediate access to design ideas for people from C&E Merchandising, Marketing, and Retail Real Estate departments at corporate headquarters. And further on in the development process, the models also proved quite useful at each store site, as the building contractors, sub-contractors, and local designers and architects supervising construction used them for visual reference.

Four views of the model for the first prototype store, eventually built in Richmond, Virginia. The architects created these 1:50 scale models out of wood, then allowed the clients to work with the moveable components to try out different floor plans and arrangements of store fixtures.

For the first prototype store, in Richmond, the KPMB designers created a wood model at a scale of 1:50. The model was fabricated at the KPMB office in Toronto, then taken to a design review meeting at the C&E headquarters in Woodstock, Connecticut. With moveable models of store components available, various alternative store layouts were set up in the model and photographed. The C&E personnel then reviewed all the floor plan options, requesting some changes. The designers then took the model back to Toronto, developed several new elements based on the client critique, and installed them. This "revised" model then became the template for the Richmond store. Once the project was completed, both client and designers analyzed every aspect of the look and operational efficiency to determine how it might be refined for future locations.

The next round of designs included prototypes for three different-sized stores: 2,400 to 2,800 square feet (216 to 252 square meters), 2,000 square feet (180 square meters), and 1,200 to 1,400 square feet (108 to 126 square meters) in size. For each model, the designers used the same kit-of-parts of furniture and display components created for the Richmond model to allow the client to view alternative layouts. Subsequently, as each store location was identified, the client would send as-built drawings for existing stores to KPMB for review, and KPMB would quickly work up a new design proposal appropriate to the new site. The proposal went to client headquarters, where a new model was then assembled out of the existing components. This model was made available for use by the local designer and general contractor for each store, to make sure they met the standards for style and construction established in the first prototype store.

Included in the second group of prototypes was the 2,400-square-foot (216-square-meter) store located in a mall in King of Prussia, Pennsylvania. As is true of all the stores, the key design qualities are the store's openness, warmth, and inviting ambience. The look represents an effort to "reinforce the core values of the retail brand, while making a contemporary impact designed to target and attract a younger customer base," notes Shirley Blumberg, who served as project architect for KPMB. The design maximizes the visible frontage with a full-height glass storefront. Inside, the plan creates a fairly open volume, with various "floating islands of merchandise." Beech fixtures and maple floors offer the warmth of wood, yet also establish a lighter, fresher atmosphere, to appeal to a younger clientele. Signature elements include the leaf-shaped, custom-designed lighting fixtures on the ceiling and similar organic forms for display tables, cabinets, and niches.

⊘ The store interior is made of maple and beech. The display tables in the room's center are meant to "float" in the space, and can be moved around. The wall fixtures are fixed, and arranged to present a "hierarchy of visual merchandising." The leaf-shaped, custom-designed lighting fixtures serve as a signature element.

⊘ Backed by tall display shelves and tea culture-related photographs and artifacts, the black tea counter at the rear of the store (left rear in photo) works as a visual anchor.

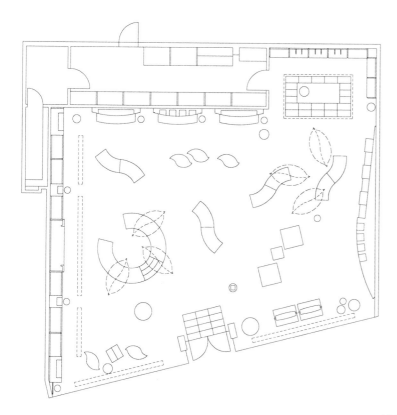

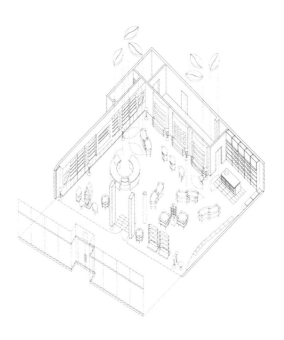

Plan and axonometric show two views of the store, with wall fixtures, flexible floor display fixtures, and lighting fixtures. The rectilinear perimeter elements are balanced by the organic, leaf-shaped curves and circles of the floating display tables and counters, and the custom lighting fixtures.

The perimeter walls feature a series of fixed display units in a range of forms designed to convey a "hierarchy of visual merchandising and presentation," notes the architect. While the curving cash/wrap desk is lightly fixed to the floor, the other fixtures floating in the center of the store are designed for mobility and flexibility. Window display units work as simple frameworks and allow seasonal display changes. Balancing all these flexible and mobile components, the tea counter in the rear of the store serves as a "highly visible anchor" with tall fixtures behind it displaying large photos of the artifacts and the culture of tea. The black tea counter, designed for tea preparation and service, enhances the sophisticated retail atmosphere by offering dramatic counterpoint to the airy display elements floating through the store.

Light, leaf-shaped display tables with thin metal legs exhibit contemporary style; the material of choice, wood, conveys a warm, inviting message.

cove landing

L.A. MORGAN

Hamburg Cove, Connecticut

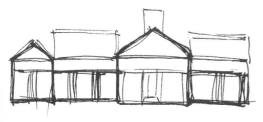

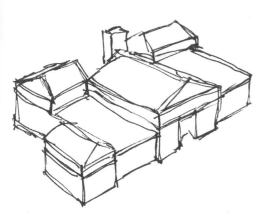

Three early sketches show the designer/owner's concept for the store, built atop a nineteenth-century foundation and including the ceiling from the original nineteenth-century building, which shaped the main central pavilion. That form inspired the proportions and shapes of the three other pavilions, linked to the rebuilt original structure with a pair of flat roofed sections.

Located along Connecticut's Eight Mile River some 100 miles from New York City, the Cove Landing antique store established itself as a destination for serious buyers almost immediately upon opening. One reason for the store's success is surely its design: the plain yet elegant wooden building and its spare, luminous interior, designed by L.A. Morgan (part owner of the store), make a perfect, highly flexible stage for the presentation and sale of fine, high-end antiques.

The original building on the site, a nineteenth-century structure long buried beneath various ramshackle additions, had at times served as a general store, gas station, butcher shop, liquor store, and soda fountain. However, the structure had been abandoned for almost 20 years, and had recently been condemned. Given an attractive site and a generous footprint of 3,300 square feet (297 square meters), Morgan elected to build on the exact same footprint, and also to integrate portions of the original foundation into the new structure. He also recycled the ceiling from the original nineteenth century, pre-addition building. That ceiling, one and a half stories above ground, included rafters made of different tree trunks (with the bark still on) and wide, rough-cut planks, all in excellent condition in spite of the disrepair elsewhere in the building. By removing the second floor in the space Morgan was able to expose the existing structure, opening a generous volume in the shell of the original building.

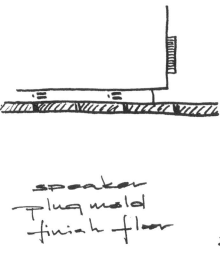

speaker
plug mold
finish floor

⊘ Detail drawings of plugmold system and
⊘ speakers; the designer's efforts go towards
minimizing any visual intrusions in the
spare, flexible spaces he creates.

Exterior views of the west terrace and
other areas reveals the simple clarity of the
design. The peaked pavilion form was generated by an existing nineteenth-century
structure on the site, then repeated in three
new pavilions linked by two flat-roofed con-
nectors. Every opening in the building is the
same size, with pocket doors to simplify
moving pieces in and out, and to create a
sense of unity in the asymmetrical structure.
Terraces can be used for entertaining clients
as well as displaying garden antiques.

The proportions of this volume then served as a kind of
template, dictating the design of the building, which
includes three similarly-scaled, high-ceilinged pavilions
connected by a pair of flat-roofed sections. Though the
resulting floor plan is asymmetrical, consistent detailing establishes a sense of unity and order, as does the
positioning of the pavilions so that they are all symmetrical on an east-west axis, while none are symmetrical
on the north-south axis.

Since the building is used primarily as a showcase for
European and Asian antiques from the seventeenth century to the twentieth century, the interiors necessarily
had to be "receptive to all periods and styles of furniture and objects," notes Morgan. To this end, he created a mix of different sized spaces, "allowing the pieces
to be viewed in appropriately scaled contexts." To
enhance the simple, spare qualities of the spaces, and
maintain consistency, he made every opening in the
building a floor-to-ceiling pocket door, and every hall
the same width. A system of plugmolds recessed at the
base of the walls and picture hanging tracks at the tops
of the walls allows items to be hung or plugged in without visible cords or holes in the walls. These features,
plus a policy of removing sold items from the floor
immediately, enhances the adaptability of the space.
Highly durable Ipe (a South American hardwood) floors
and Swedish putty-sanded walls provide a quiet, non-
intrusive, and easily maintained backdrop for the pieces
on display.

Given an upscale clientele that travels for two hours or more to reach the store, the design included a provision for a full kitchen for catering on site. The entire kitchen can be hidden behind panels if necessary, and its look is consistent with the store: even the sink is a dove-tailed wooden box set on slab of marble that serves as a counter. An outdoor terrace located between three of the pavilions provides space for entertaining as well as displaying garden antiques. The client bathroom is a sculpted cube made of sandblasted glass, which filters in light yet maintains the uninterrupted sense of flow between the various spaces. Every room on the main floor is accessible to the store's patrons; the "back-of-house" spaces thus share the same spare, elegant look as the showrooms, while all the mechanical and other systems, from vent ducts to light switches, are hidden to minimize visual distraction.

Moving through the various volumes of the store is an experience in shifting perspectives, as one goes from room to room, from low to high, from narrow to open, with the circulation organized to provide appealing visual vignettes of the merchandise on display. The background perfectly complements the objects, which pretty much defines success in retail design—as does a volume of business that exceeds projections. Such has been the case at Cove Landing since opening day.

⊗ This view lends a sense of the rigorousness of the interior architecture, with its pleasingly symmetrical proportions and absence of clutter. The floor of Ipe wood and walls of Swedish sanded putty provide a quiet backdrop for the antiques, arranged for dramatic effect. A plugmold system at the base of the walls eliminates the clutter of wires.

⊗ A fireplace adds a pleasant residential touch to the store, two hours from New York and thus quite a trek for most of its city-based patrons. All the openings in the building's walls are the same size, enhancing the sense of unity and right proportion.

The bathroom is screened from the store by walls of translucent sandblasted glass, permitting privacy yet allowing light to flow through. The owner/designer installed a bathroom and kitchen because the store is relatively isolated, and most clients drive a hundred miles from New York to get there.

Owner/designer L.A. Morgan created this sunny office for himself in the store.

Augustus the bull terrier finds a sunny spot in a Cove Landing hallway to his liking. Note how the walls don't quite reach the ceiling—the space between serves as a track for hanging pictures.

gene juarez salon

NBBJ

Seattle, Washington

Working on the premise that a facility dedicated to making people beautiful should itself be beautiful, NBBJ has crafted a series of warm, colorfully appealing spaces, each dedicated to a specific element of the salon and spa experience. Located in an understated Modernist building in downtown Seattle, this day spa/salon offers patrons a serene, soothing retreat, "a place of uplifting beauty, with exquisite details everywhere," according to Rysia Suchecka, of NBBJ's interiors design team. Yet there is more to the Juarez spa than well-crafted space: Suchecka for years has been a serious student of design history, with a special interest in the Roman floor mosaics called cosmati, a style prevalent from the ninth to the thirteenth centuries.

Suchecka's interpretations of the hypnotic, entrancing floor patterns found in myriad Roman churches from that period are in evidence in the waiting and retail areas of the Juarez spa, appropriately scaled to match the spaces and the ceiling heights. As Suchecka notes: "I always like the floors in the old Roman churches. In a simple volume, you see the floor. People don't look up when they're walking through a space, they look down. The floor is important." Not many patrons of this fresh, contemporary facility will recognize the source of inspiration for the floors, but no matter: the design gracefully and subtly integrates the old influences into the new interior to make timelessly beautiful space.

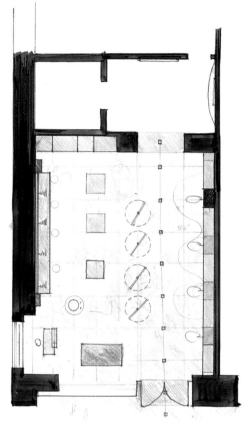

The designers tried several different layouts for the ground-floor plan.

Drawing shows the floor plan for a water feature in the spa.

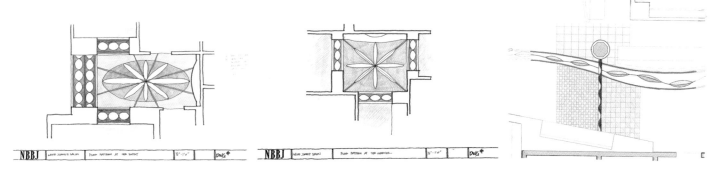

⊘ Groups of drawings and detailed plans show how the floor patterns for the spa entrance, corridors, and reception area are first designed and developed, then specified for installation.

⊘ Street level plan shows retail shop in corner of the building. The upper level houses the salon and spa. The curving wall defines the passage from the parking garage/elevator into the facility. A row of pedicure tables flanks the curving wall. The salon rooms occupy the perimeter at bottom and right, with the more intimate spa treatment rooms in the core.

The geometrically-patterned floors set the tone, foundation for a series of distinct spatial experiences that begins with the retail area on the street level, finished with a hand-plastered interior walls, travertine marble floors, and dark wood shelving for spa products. Glass shelving and drawers display hair products, while pivoting bronze frame panels offer transparent photographic images advertising salon services.

While the street level serves as the ostensible primary entrance, accessing the reception and retail space and the elevator banks that send patrons up to the salon's main level, most patrons arrive from the parking garage and its secondary entrance. To make the journey from garage to spa and salon more appealing (and to help separate the manicure area, with its strong-smelling nail polishes, from the rest of the spa) the designers created a 55-foot-long (16.5-meter-long), sinuously curving, hand-cast glass wall to define the passage. Suchecka attributes inspiration for this element to the translucent, evanescent snow sculptures of artist Andy Goldworthy. Establishing an ethereal, foggy atmosphere, the wall

guides patrons with a visual dance of shadows and light; once inside, patrons relax in waiting areas designed like living rooms, with cast stone fireplaces, wood shelves, warm lighting, and accessories and artworks selected for residential appeal.

Suchecka specified three distinct water features, in the entry, at the termination of the treatment room corridor, and in a waiting area, to create the soothing, gentle sounds that enhance the spa experience. The treatment rooms feature bamboo floors, hand-painted walls with botanical themes, and sculpted wall niches for accessories.

The designers created three distinct, richly-finished water features to add visual richness as well as soothing sounds to the spa.

With custom furnishings, fireplaces, and fine artworks and accessories, the spa waiting areas offer patrons a quietly luxurious residential-style experience. The floor patterns are inspired by floors in the ninth- to thirteenth-century style called cosmati, which designer Rysia Suchecka studied in Europe.

In developing the shelving and display systems, the advertising display panels, and other components, the designers draw multiple images of the retail shop interiors.

⊗ Designer Suchecka created a series of custom display tables for the retail shop.

⊗ Treatment rooms feature a variety of colors and textures, establishing different moods for different types of treatments.

Within the hair salon, the walls are made of fabric, offering a soft, soothing embrace—and the flexibility to be changed seasonally, to enhance the theatrical aspect of the experience. As Suchecka notes, "a visit to the salon is a kind of transformation, not unlike the theater, and so we made walls that can be changed, like sets, with the seasons." Floor colors also change from room to room, to support different palettes. Custom furniture and fabric-wrapped lighting fixtures enrich the visual and tactile appeal of the diverse spaces. Cutting stations feature wood with glass shelves, while the technical area reflects its function with a high-tech look established with stainless and plastic laminate.

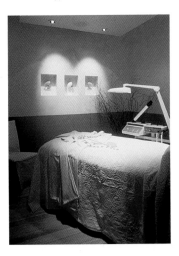

⊗ The inspiration for the mosaic floors came from a style prevalent in the late Roman empire, from the ninth to thirteenth centuries, called cosmati.

planned parenthood
golden gate clinics

FOUGERON ARCHITECTURE

Oakland, California

The designers built in security, with bullet-resistant glass in front of the reception desk.

With bombings and shootings from anti-choice fanatics a possibility at any time, and confrontations ranging from passive to violent an ever-present reality, family planning clinics in the United States generate a different set of design issues than those common to most health care facilities. Along with the usual medical issues, security and safety have become paramount at clinics providing birth control counseling and especially abortion services. Yet when the operators of the Planned Parenthood Golden Gate clinic, located in the low-income, ethnically mixed neighborhood of South Oakland, elected to do a security upgrade on their 5,000-square-foot (450-square-meter) facility, they decided to improve on comfort and aesthetics as well.

Therese Wilson, chapter vice president for marketing and public affairs, commissioned and worked with architect Margaret Fougeron on the project. In addition to specifying low-cost paneled screens and brightly colored new seating to cheer up the interiors and creating a new graphics program to replace the clutter of posted papers, Fougeron (a committed believer in the right to choose) had to research less glamorous—and very expensive—subjects like bullet-resistant materials for the reception area. Reaction to the newly refurbished

At the new Eastmont clinic a waiting room with steel-framed rice-paper panels, skylights, and comfortable, low-cost furnishings establish a warm, calm, and friendly ambience.

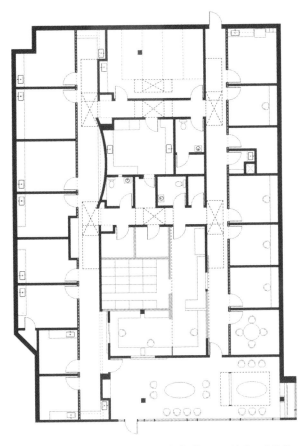

Plan of the Eastmont clinic, with the reception/waiting area at bottom right. The basic plan is a U-shape, with offices, exam rooms, and counseling rooms accessed from the corridor. At upper left, a curving section of corridor wall makes a small seating area for staff and clients.

clinic was strongly positive—so positive that the clinic's directors saw a need for a larger space. They moved the 15-year-old facility to a new 7,000-square-foot (630-square-meter) space in a mall, and hired Fougeron, now officially on board as Planned Parenthood's affiliate architect, to plan the new clinic.

To help ease the emotionally charged issues around family planning, the new clinic offers a warm, bright, and calm environment, bathed in natural light from sky-lights with canted shafts and from clerestory windows screened with colored and sandblasted glass. Privacy is another important issue in family planning clinics; here, the designers sandblasted the clinic's glass storefront, to protect privacy yet maintain a sense of openness and transparency. The floor plan is U-shaped, with eight exam rooms, three nurses' stations, two offices, two counseling rooms, and a staff lounge organized along both the perimeter and in the core of a U-shaped circu-lation corridor. The entry and waiting area has been fit-ted with low-maintenance sealed cork tiles, and offers the clinic's clients the much-needed amenity of a chil-dren's play area—a space delineated by steel-framed panels made of rice-paper laminates and polycarbonate infills. The architect added one other lively note by curving one corridor wall, painting it red, and building in an informal seat for clients and staff. Fougeron developed a graphics program for the clinic as well, and created a framing system so that staff can post notices in hinged frames on the waiting room wall.

⊘ Elevations shows how the
⊘ clinic is bathed in light from
a pair of steeply raked
skylights.

Rather than go the usual route of hiring a guard and installing a metal detector and lockers, the operators of the Golden Gate clinic asked Fougeron to design and build security into the facility. As has been made clear it is not the patients but the doctors, nurses, and staff personnel that are under threat of violence, and so the designers installed bullet-resistant laminate glass over the reception window, with a half-inch air space to allow voices to be heard. The treatment areas are accessed by doors with electric locks provided with buzzer releases.

As is evident in the photographs, the design of the new and original clinics works as intended, helping its low-income clients obtain a sense of dignity, comfort, and respect while dealing with the often painful and difficult issues of family planning.

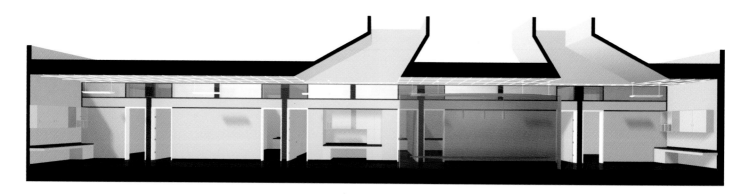

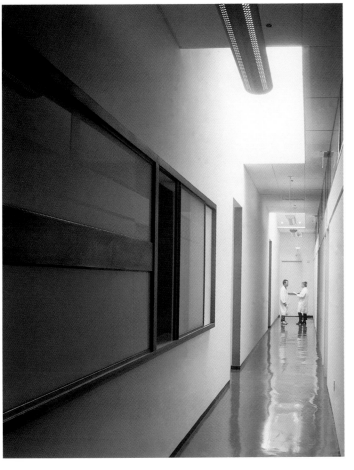

 The clinics' environment is warm, bright, and calm and highly secure.

county of alameda self sufficiency center

MICHAEL WILLIS ARCHITECTS

Oakland, California

Welfare recipients encounter a pleasant, light-filled reception area.

Natural light floods into the skylit rotunda at the employment services intake area.

An interior that conveys a sense of optimism and dignity can lift the spirits of a welfare recipient, yet most welfare office are dreary, worn-out places. Not so the prototype for the Self Sufficiency Centers for the County of Alameda, California. Designed by Michael Willis, the center is a welcoming collection of offices radiating off a light-filled "town square."

In response to recent welfare reforms, the County of Alameda will be instituting a series of Self Sufficiency Centers to help welfare recipients return to the workforce. Each center will offer a wide range of support programs in a one-stop facility located near public transportation. The prototype designed by Michael Willis Architects is at the Eastmont Town Center, the former Eastmont Mall where the county has already developed a health clinic and is working with local retails and nonprofit organizations to revive stores and other services.

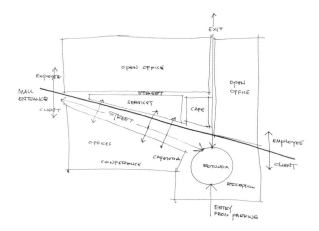

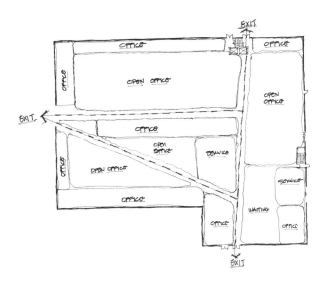

The county obtained a former department store for the center, the interior spaces of which receive little daylight. To brighten the interiors, the architect placed the main reception and childcare areas toward an outdoor courtyard, which was the department store's garden center. A rotunda near the facility's center acts as a "town square," the primary organizing device for the client services area inside. A light monitor illuminates the rotunda, drawing in clients as they enter from the parking lot or the mall. Private offices for counsels and services, such as "Dress for Success," are located here. Client-oriented spaces also include a cafeteria, computer and telephone banks, and conference rooms for training, counseling, and meeting with potential employees.

County workers are located in a secure area adjacent to the client services. A series of large "streets" organize the space and create visual interest. At the intersection of these streets is the staff's own "town square," or lounge, which can accommodate large meetings. A simple garage door can separate the space into smaller meeting rooms when desired. Curving walls along the streets contribute to the dynamic quality of the staff's offices.

Preliminary and final floor plans show architect's concern with establishing a clear pathway from the reception atrium through the center.

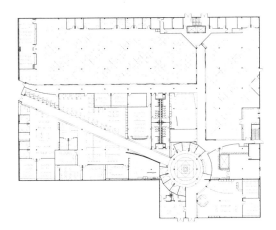

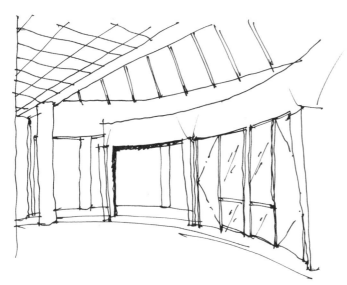

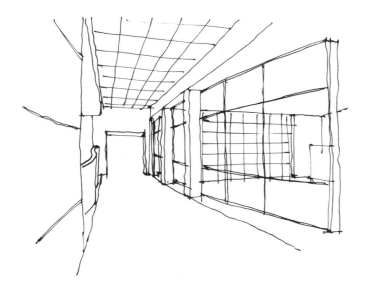

⊘ A separate cafeteria provides meals for county employees.

⊘ The architect's conceptual sketches for the "town square."

The client cafeteria provides a congenial yet semi-private dining space.

View from the mall entry toward the rotunda reveals the architect's use of bold, geometric forms.

Daycare is provided for children of the welfare recipients receiving assistance.

The client phone bank offers privacy.

A cheery intake reception area for assistance services.

swedish covenant hospital

EVA MADDOX ASSOCIATES; O'DONNELL, WICKLUND, PIGOZZI & PATTERSON, ARCHITECTS OF RECORD.
Chicago, Illinois

SWEDISH HERITAGE

⊘ Eva Maddox Associates reviewed Swedish design patterns as early research for the hospital interiors.

⊘ In addition, the team explored symbols and objects that were considered multicultural to match the make-up of the institution's staff and patients.

MULTI-CULTURAL CELEBRATION

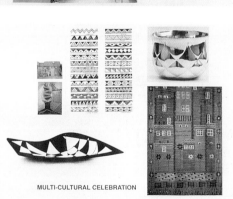

MULTI-CULTURAL CELEBRATION

Sign language and symbolism become the tools used for solving the contradictory interests of the client. The hospital wished to convey its Judeo-Christian, Swedish heritage and at the same time embrace its status as a multicultural, community care center. Eva Maddox Associates approached the problem with its established method of "patterning," and created a cheerful, user-friendly complex that embraces the hospital's holistic approach to healing the body, mind, and spirit.

Eva Maddox Associates was hired to upgrade 125,00-square-feet (11,250-square-meters) of this 185,000-square-foot (16,650-square-meter) health-care complex. The center provides outpatient cancer treatment, surgical procedures and family medical treatment. Through "patterning," Eva Maddox begins by "evaluating the nature of any given project and overlaying memory patterns that relate to the client's identity within a given spatial framework."

For the Swedish Covenant Hospital, extensive research revealed characteristics that would provide a Scandinavian flavor to the interiors. Materials, such as stone, textile fibers, and woods. The brickwork used extensively in Swedish construction is applied externally and reappears inside the lobby and continues in the elevator banks, restrooms, and stairwell. Colors were borrowed from the Swedish flag: blue and yellow are used throughout the interiors. The blond-colored wood is often identified with Scandinavian furniture.

1ST FLOOR COLOR DISTRIBUTION PLAN

⊗ First floor offices and departments radiate off the central rotunda, as seen in the first floor plan.

⊗ Floor plan detail of the first floor rotunda shows the symbolic markings on the floor, which are predominately in the Swedish colors of blue and yellow.

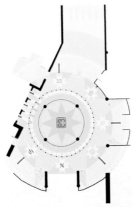

First Floor Rotunda

Swedish Covenant Hospital

Dominant to the interiors is a circular pattern, which is first witnessed in the grand rotunda. The circular is meant to convey the Judeo-Christian heritage and be symbolic of the "continuum of life." The circle pattern is repeated elsewhere in the floor plan on a smaller scale. Given the hospital's location in a multicultural city like Chicago, its staff and patients speak as many as 30 different languages. So, to embrace that polyglot culture, the designer expanded the use of graphic symbols for wayfinding and signage. Drawn as spirals, stars, waves, lozenges, and more, these symbols are translated to mean wind, rain, and water. They direct the visitor through the hospital.

Overall, the interior upgrade and image components encompassed a mere one-half of one percent of the project's $40 million budget.

⊗ The wayfinding and signage system was consistent throughout the floors.

⊗ A warm white light illuminates the upper tier rotunda.

⊗ The rotunda, as seen from above. The midpoint design is the Swedish Covenant's logo monogram, which the inverted exclamation marks and the saw-toothed bar are decorative patterns taken from Scandinavian textiles. Swirl-within-star denotes life force.

⊗ Model of the rotunda complete with floor pattern mentioned above.

FIRST FLOOR

FIFTH FLOOR

SECOND FLOOR

SIXTH FLOOR

THIRD FLOOR

SEVENTH FLOOR

 Symbols used on floors in addition to the rotunda floor.

 Elevation drawings of the main lobby, registration, and diagnostics area.

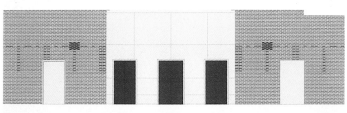

MAIN LOBBY

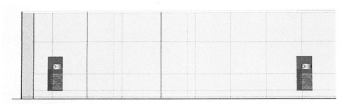

REGISTRATION

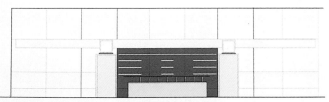

DIAGNOSTICS

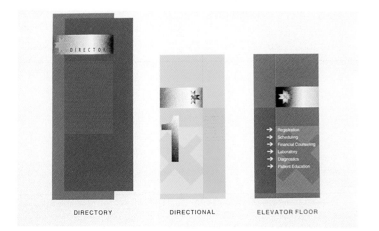

DIRECTORY   DIRECTIONAL   ELEVATOR FLOOR

⊗ Photograph of the rotunda with all its elements in
place.

⊙ View of the patient's registration area. Blue flooring
strips are direction pointers that lead to information
centers.

⊗ On the second floor, surgery recovery areas.

⊗ Example of the signage system.

padre serra catholic church

A.C. MARTIN & ASSOCIATES

Camarillo, California

⊘ View of the church complex, with the octagonal sanctuary building in foreground. The architecture draws on Jewish and Native American, as well as Spanish Colonial, traditions.

⊘ The spare, cubist quality of the building has a modern look to it, but the thick-walled look is also consistent with the traditional southwestern/Spanish approach of building with adobe.

Rejecting the traditional architecture of the Church, A.C. Martin & Associates instead turned to a myriad of influences when designing the Padre Serra Catholic Church. Incorporating numerous cultural, liturgical, and historical traditions, by design the church serves all the necessary functions; and yet is subtly infused with the magisterial sense of mystery that is a fundamental element of organized spiritual experience.

Named for the priest who founded Catholic missions up and down the California coast over 200 years ago, the Padre Serra Catholic Church in Camarillo (a small but rapidly growing agricultural town north of Los Angeles) draws not only on the Spanish colonial-influenced seminary designs of Father Serra but also on the liturgical architecture of the Jewish faith and Native American design. As architect David Martin explains, "the genesis of the symmetrically-generated plan was inspired by ancient Jewish temples that were octagonal in plan." Covering nearly 12 acres of ground bounded on three sides by a large agricultural plain, the church complex has been designed as a metaphorical village, centered around a Mediterranean-style courtyard that will function as a gathering place before and after church services. To temper the often-intense California light, the church's apertures are mostly small in scale, and the larger ones have been screened with olive trees on the outside.

A Mediterranean-style courtyard fronts the church entrance, functioning as an outdoor gathering place before and after services.

The bell tower, seen across the courtyard from the church interior, strikes a traditional Spanish note, enhanced by the red tile roofs.

Side view of the baptismal font, with a starry night sky painted overhead—the heavens, first sight seen for the newly baptized.

Views over the font into the sanctuary. The altar is located in the center, beneath the skylight framed by timbers in the upper reaches of the dome. Large, Mission-style chandeliers help scale down the space as well as enhance the daylight. The central location of the altar puts the presider in close contact with worshippers—an arrangement that grew out of the Vatican II guidelines which set out to make the church more accessible and less formal.

For all its grounding in tradition, the church sanctuary interiors display a more contemporary look, influenced above all by the Vatican II guidelines that stress the participation of worshippers. It was Vatican II that began the ritual of masses held in native languages and set out to make the relationship between congregation and clergy less formal—to make the presider, as representative of the church, more accessible. At the Serra Church, this has been accomplished by placing the altar in the center of sanctuary, beneath a skylit dome, rather than the front. This places worshippers on all sides of the altar, within 40 feet (12 meters) of the presider. The altar lies on axis with the baptismal font and the narthex.

From the entry, the narthex or gathering place, the main axis leads through a double row of columns, past the baptismal font, and on to the altar. Above the font, a painting of a starry nighttime sky—the heavens—becomes the first image seen by a person after baptism. The altar is constructed of seven tons of California granite, centered in the sanctuary, and lit by a 16-foot (48-meter) square skylight framed by intersecting arches of timber. Theatrical spots enhance the daylight when required. Chandeliers serve as decorations and light sources, and also help to scale down the high ceilings.

A view across the font through the narthex, or entrance, framed by heavy columns.

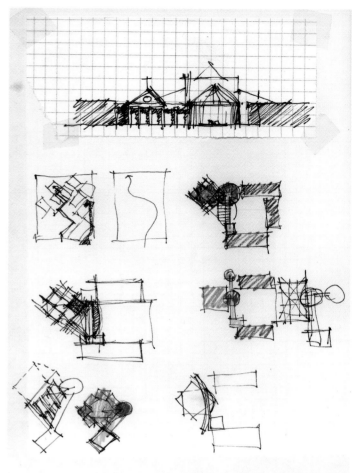

Color and black and white studies for the floor plan and elevation.

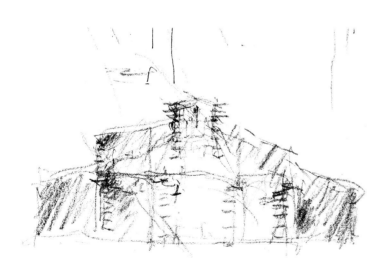

Rough early sketch of the building.

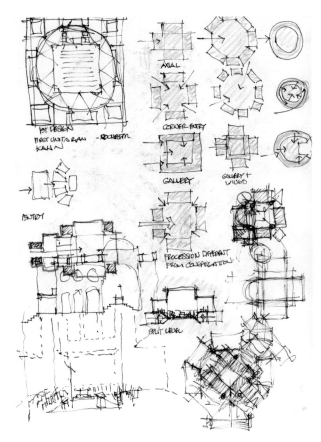

⊗ Color and black and white studies for the floor plans and various sections of the interior.

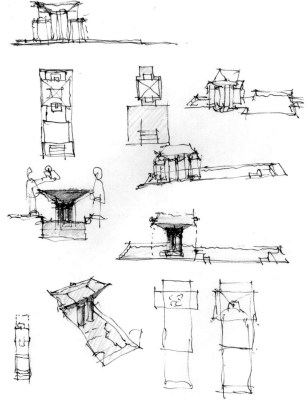

⊗ Baptismal font studies.

⊗ Studies for the sanctuary and other interior elements.

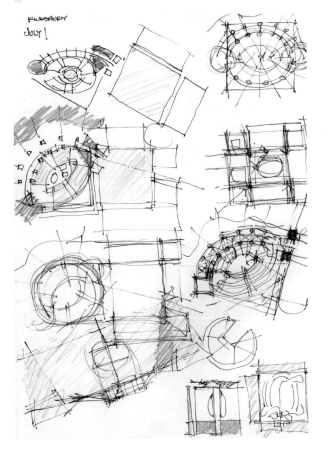

university hall, new york university

DAVIS BRODY BOND

New York, New York

⊘ A translucent glass wall screens the servery from the two-story dining hall.

⊘ The sloped, tensile-structure skylight allows an abundance of natural light to enter the dining hall, and in turn disguises its location as a windowless basement.

New York University needed to create student housing quickly, yet wanted that housing to be more sophisticated than the typical dormitory space. Equally challenging was the location—a site at a major thoroughfare near the city's Union Square, a "special" district with specific zoning requirements. Overcoming these obstacles, Davis Brody Bond's University Hall is so successful that now, at the end of each term, students virtually have to be ordered to move out and find housing elsewhere in the city. Given the exorbitant cost of housing in Manhattan, it is nearly impossible for them to find accommodations of such quality.

The goal was to provide a "warm and stylish" place where students and faculty could socialize informally as well as reside. The 200,000-square-foot (18,000-square-meter) U-shaped tower contains many common amenities, such as a laundry and exercise rooms, library, recreational facilities, and dining room. The majority of the apartments in the 20-story building are four-person suites with two bedrooms, kitchen, bath, and living room. To set the interior's mood, in the common rooms and public areas warm-toned and durable materials were chosen, including terrazzo floors, jura stone and maple walls, stainless steel and glass.

A terrazzo staircase leads down to the airy cafeteria, where students linger over their meals.

The general public, as well as students, are welcome in the ground-floor coffee bar.

To maintain the retail orientation of the street, the ground floor features a café and bookstore announced by an open canopy. The second to fourteenth floors of the building have a pre-cast concrete façade with a varied pattern of windows and protruding sills providing a playful break in the façade. The remaining floors are set back, above the required street wall and are clad in a glass and metal curtain wall that glows at night.

The most unique space is the two-story dining hall that is covered by a sloped, tensile-structured skylight. The cafeteria is a light-filled, welcoming space surrounded on two sides by a landscaped garden, despite the fact that it is set below ground level. This room is also used to host special functions, such as banquets, meetings, and receptions. A wall of translucent glass screens the servery from the main eating area.

Compliance with local zoning mandated retail activity at street level. The architect solved this problem by adding a storefront café and bookstore, which opens the building to the public and makes it a more friendly neighbor. Careful scaling and detailing of the exterior makes the building's exterior distinctive while remaining consistent with the overall style of the neighborhood.

⊘ The dining hall is flanked on two sides by landscaped gardens.

The translucent glass wall allows screened views into the dining hall.

chicago state university student union building

EVA MADDOX ASSOCIATES; HARRY WEESE, ARCHITECT OF RECORD
WITH JOHN & LEE ARCHITECTS, ASSOCIATE ARCHITECT
Chicago, Illinois

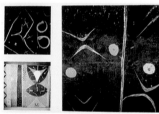

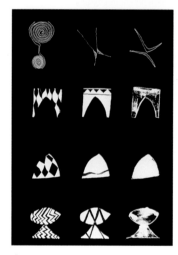

Sources for "patterning" research for student union building. Most symbols were found in textiles and carvings.

A minority institution of higher learning, Chicago State University celebrates its ethnicity, pride, and heritage—and wanted to portray this in its new student union building. The college, headed by Dr. Dolores Cross, turned to Eva Maddox Associates, to develop a one-of-a-kind, central gathering place for students and facility that could be a learning, as well as a gathering, place The goal was to "visually link the university to its special character." The skylit, two-story rotunda, in fact, has become a vivid and powerful symbol at the heart of the 161-acre campus.

The center's cone-shaped, steel and glass atrium roof sleekly recalls traditional thatched dwellings in Africa. Yet, it is interiors that explode with symbolism. This is not surprising for design by this group, for Eva Maddox typically sees the "need for a building's interior to incorporate metaphorical resonances." In the 62,000-square-foot (5,580-square-meter) student center, Eva Maddox Associates linked past to present through the use of theological and philosophical proverbs. These

The designers relied on Adinkra symbols taken from ancient Ghana for their research.

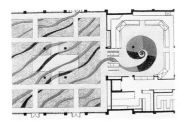

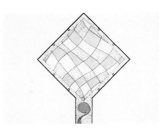

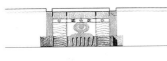

Sketches of possible floor patterns.

Sketches of symbols used in the cafeteria area.

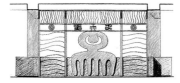

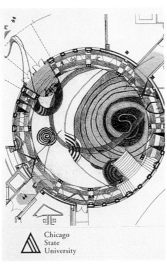

Chicago State University

Sketches of the hallway and restroom entrance.

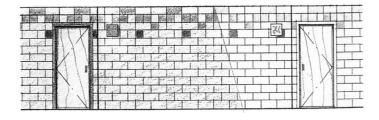

proverbs are seen as graphic patterns taken from ancient Ghana textiles and carvings called Adinkra—20 different images discovered by researchers that bespeak of ethnicity, pride, heritage, and sense of place to the 9,000 CSU students. They selected images that could be transferred verbatim to the walls for flooring or extracted or adapted for the university's promotion and teaching materials.

The Adinkra images are interpreted by bricks laid in conventional or African house construction style. Some images are inserted in terrazzo flooring and painted onto metal dividers that are themselves shaped into Adinkra forms. Fabrics are applied to offsight tackboards and work station partitions in the offices consist of black and white cotton mud cloth.

The hugely successful heart and hub of the campus, the vividly decorated student union is where students and faculty gather for performances, lectures, exhibits and social and academic events, and is aptly situated on Martin Luther King Drive.

Rotunda terrazzo floor—work in progress.

The interior structuring of the rotunda shows the work of architects Harry Weese and Johns and Lee and focuses on stairs, columns, trusswork, and conical top with skylight. Semiotic flooring pattern is an abstraction of Adinkra symbol.

The dining area with Adinkra symbol of painted metal treated as part of the floor-to-ceiling grille. The dominant image is the symbol of feminine power, love, and working together in the community.

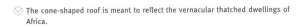
The dominant metal grille in this part of the cafeteria is the symbol of readiness to be called to arms.

View of the offices with Afro-centric patterned material on sofa and mud-cloth work station partitions.

The cone-shaped roof is meant to reflect the vernacular thatched dwellings of Africa.

directory of firms

Randy Brown Architects
6704 Dodge St.
Omaha, Nebraska 68132
Phone: 402-551-7097
fax 402-551-2033
Randy Brown Studio/Residence
Broadmoor Development

Carr Design Group
49 Exhibition Street
Melbourne, Victoria 3000
Australia
Phone: 613-9654-8692
fax 613-9650-5002
Santos SAOABU Headquarters

Caruzzo Rancati Riva
Architetti Associati
Via Pergolesi, 2
20124 Milan, Italy
Phone: 02-6671-3092 or
02-6671-3-70
fax 02-6749-0566
Protti Apartment
Ghais Apartment

Cecconi Simone Inc.
1335 Dudas Street, West
Toronto, Ontario
Canada M6J 1Y3
Phone: 416-588-5900
fax 416-462-2577
Modern Living Space
Private Office

Davis Brody Bond
315 Hudson Street
New York, New York 10013
Phone: 212-633-4700
fax 212-633-4762
The Children's Place
  Headquarters
University Hall,
  New York University

Di Leonardo International
2350 Post Road, Suite 1
Warwick, Rhode Island
02886-2242
Phone: 401-732-2900
fax 401-732-5315
Chelsea Millennium Hotel
Le Merigot Beach Hotel & Spa

Mary Douglas Drysdale Design
1733 Connecticut Avenue, NW
Washington, DC 20009
Phone: 202-588-0700
Pennsylvania Farm House

Steven Ehrlich Architects
10865 Washington Blvd.
Culver City, California 90232
Phone: 310-838-9700
fax 310-838-9737
Woods Residence
Ten8Sixty-Five Architects' Office

Faulding Architects/F2Design
11 East 22nd Street
New York, New York 10010
Phone: 212-253-1513
fax 212-253-9711
Townhouse R

Fougeron Architects
3537 21st Street
San Francisco, California 94114
Phone: 415-641-5744
fax 415-282-6434
Kuhling/Wilcox Residence
Planned Parenthood
  Golden Gate Clinics

GGLO Architecture
and Interior Design
1191 Second Avenue, Suite 1650
Seattle, Washington 98101-3426
Phone: 206-467-6828
fax 206-467-0627
Gaylord Residence Remodel
Grinstein Residence
  Bathroom Remodel
My Garage & Studio

Hodgetts + Fung Design
Associates
5837 Adams Blvd.
Culver City, California 90232
Phone: 323-937-2150
fax 323-937-2151
American Cinematheque
  at the Egyptian Theater

Huntsman Architectural Group
465 California Street, Suite 1000
San Francisco, California 94104
Phone: 415-394-1212
fax 415-394-1222
300 California Street
Learn It!

Koning Eizenberg Architects
1454 25th Street
Santa Monica, California 90404
Phone: 310-828-6131
fax 310-828-0719
Avalon Hotel
Rare Medium Offices

Kuwabara Payne McKenna
Blumberg
322 King Street West
Toronto, Ontario, Canada
M5V 1J2
Phone: 416-977-5104
fax 416-598-9840
Crabtree & Evelyn

David Ling Architects
225 E. 21st Street
New York, New York 10010
Phone: 212-982-7089
fax 212-475-1336
Cabana Postproduction Facilities

Eva Maddox Associates, Inc.
300 West Hubbard Street
Chicago, Illinois 60610
Phone: 312-321-1151
Chicago State University
  Student Union
Swedish Covenant Hospital

Mahlum Architects
71 Columbia Street, Suite 400
Seattle, Washington 98104
Phone: 206-441-4151
fax 206-441-0478
Doc Martens
The Pearl District Offices
  of Mahlum Architects

A.C. Martin Partners
811 West Seventh Street,
5th floor
Los Angeles, California
90017-3408
Phone: 213-683-1900
fax 213-614-6002
Padre Serra Catholic Church

L.A. Morgan
Post Office Box 39
Hadlyme, Connecticut 06439
Phone: 860-434-0304
fax 860-434-3103
Tribeca Loft
Cove Landing Antique Store

NBBJ Architects
111 South Jackson Street
Seattle, Washington 98104
Phone: 206-223-5555
fax 206-621-2300
Edmond Meany Hotel
Gene Juarez Salon

Olson/Sundberg Architects
108 First Avenue South
Seattle, Washington 98104
Phone: 206-624-5670
fax 206-624-5730
Atherton Residence
Bobo Residence

PNB
135 W. 17th Street
New York, New York 10013
Phone: 212-691-9980
fax 212-675-5939
Ideya Restaurant

Ivan Rijavec Architects
4 Wood Street
Fitzroy Victoria 3065 Australia
Phone: 613-9417-6942
fax 613-9416-0319
Alessio Residence

Rios Associates
8008 West 3rd Street
Los Angeles, California 90048
Phone: 323-852-6717
fax 323-852-6719
Rock Restaurant

Rockwell Group
5 Union Square West
New York, New York 10003
Phone: 212-463-0334
fax 212-463-0335
W Hotel
Next Door Nobu

Gisela Stromeyer Designs
165 Duane Street
New York, New York 10013
Phone/fax: 212-406-9452
Club Incognito

Clive Wilkinson Architects
101 S. Robertson Blvd.
Suite 204
Los Angeles, California 90048
Phone: 310-248-1090
TWBA/Chiat/Day West
  Coast Headquarters

Michael Willis Architects
246 1st St., Suite 200
San Francisco, California 94105
Phone: 415-957-2750
fax 415-957-2780
Alameda County Self
  Sufficiency Center
Glide Community House

WoHa Designs
135 Bukah Timah Road
Singapore 229838
Phone: 65-734-9663
fax 65-734-9662
Emerald Hill Residence
Singapore Residence

photography credits

Aker/Zvonkovic Photography,
Houston, Texas
Padre Serra Catholic Church;
p. 194, 195, 196

**Farshid Assassi/Assassi
Productions**
*Randy Brown Studio and
Residence;*
p. 66, 67, 68, 69
Edmond Meany Hotel;
p. 78, 79, 80, 81
*Broadmoor Development
Company;*
p. 127, 128, 129
Gene Juarez Salon;
p. 178, 180, 181

Richard Barnes
Kuhling/Wilcox Residence;
p. 15, 16, 17
*Planned Parenthood Golden Gate
Clinics,*
p. 182, 183, 185

Tom Bonner
Rock Restaurant;
p. 106, 108, 109
*American Cinematheque at
Egyptian Theater;*
p. 114, 115, 116

Earl Carter
Santos SAOABU;
p. 123, 124, 125

Eduardo Calderon
*Grinstein Residence Bathroom
Remodel;*
p. 63, 64, 65

Benny Chan
*TBWA/Chiat/Day West Coast
Headquarters;*
p. 131
Rare Medium Offices;
p. 135, 136, 137

Grey Crawford/ Beateworks
Avalon Hotel;
p. 88, 89

Pete Eckert
Bobo Residence;
p. 6, 7 (top),
Pearl District Office;
p. 148, 149

Pieter Estersohn
Tribecca Loft;
p. 59, 60, 61

Tim Griffith
Emerald Hill Residence;
p. 30, 31, 32, 33

Steve Hall, Hedrich Blessing
Swedish Covenant Hospital,
p. 191, 193
*Chicago State University Student
Union Building;*
p. 202, 204, 205

Robert G. Hill
Crabtree & Evelyn Store (models);
p. 170, 171

Hodgetts + Fung
American Cinematheque,
p. 114, 115, 116

James F. Housel
Gaylord Residence Remodel;
  p. 46, 48, 49

Timothy Hursley
Glide Community House;
p. 70, 71, 73

Warren Jagger
Le Merigot Beach Hotel and Spa;
p. 90, 91, 92, 93

Ken Kirkwood
Chelsea Millennium Hotel;
p. 82, 83

Albert Lim
Singapore Residence;
p. 34, 35, 36

John Linden
Woods Residence;
p. 18, 20, 21

Andrew Lautman
Pennsylvania Farm House;
p. 26, 27, 28

Douglas Levere
Ideya Restaurant;
p. 102, 103, 104, 105

Mark Luthringer
Learn IT!;
p. 158, 159, 160, 161

Michael Mundy
Cove Landing;
p. 175, 176, 177

Stuart O'Sullivan
Townhouse R;
p. 38, 39, 40, 41

Jim Olson
Atherton;
p. 13 (second from bottom)

Peter Paige
Crabtree & Evelyn Store;
p. 170, 172, 173

Alberto Piovano
Protti Apartment;
p. 51, 52, 53

Marvin Rand
Ten8Sixty-Five Architects' Office;
p. 143, 144, 145

Rijavec Architects
Alessio Residence;
p. 22, 23, 24, 25

Cesar Rubio
Postrio;
p. 110, 113

Antonio Maniscalco
Ghaiss Apartment;
p. 55, 56, 57

Michael Shopenn
My Garage Studio & Office;
p. 162, 163, 164

Andrew Mowbrey Stephenson
Townhouse R;
p. 38, 39

Holly Stickley Photography
*Doc Martens Airwair USA
Headquarters Office;*
p. 155, 156, 157

Bruce Van Inwegen
Atherton Residence;
p. 12, 13 (top, middle left)

Joy Von Tiedemann
Modern Living Space;
p. 42, 43, 44, 45
Private Office, Toronto;
p. 118, 119, 120

David Wakely
300 California Street;
p. 150, 152
*County of Alameda Self
Sufficiency Center;*
p. 186, 188, 189

Paul Warchol
Bobo Residence;
p. 7 (middle, bottom right, bottom left), 8, 9
Atherton Residence;
p. 13 (second from top, bottom)
W Hotel New York;
p. 74, 75, 76, 77
Club Incognito;
p. 96, 97
Next Door Nobu,
p. 99, 100, 101
Cabana Postproduction Facility;
p. 138, 140, 141
Children's Place;
167, 168, 169
University Hall;
p. 198, 199, 200, 201

about the authors

Justin Henderson has written four previous books for Rockport Publishers—*Workplaces and Workspaces, Museum Architecture, Casino Design,* and *Jungle Luxe,* a book on eco-lodges and indigenous-style hotels. He also wrote *Roland Terry Northwest Master Architect* for the University of Washington Press, and *San Francisco Museum of Modern Art,* written for the museum. He worked as an editor at *Interiors Magazine* for ten years, and has written for various national and regional publications in the fields of architecture, interior design, and travel. Henderson lives in Seattle, Washington, with his wife, photographer Donna Day, his daughter Jade, and Paco the poodle.

Nora Richter Greer is a freelance author/editor who has written about architecture for over 20 years. She began her career at *Architecture* magazine. She is the contributor to numerous publications and books on architecture and design, and authored *Architecture Transformed* (Rockport Publishers), co-authored *Architecture as Response* (Rockport Publishers), and *The Right Light* (Rockport Publishers), and authored *The Search for Shelter* (The AIA Press), and *The Creation of Shelter* (The AIA Press). She resides in Washington, D.C.

Rysia Suchecka is a principal at NBBJ Architects in Seattle, Washington. Her Interiors Studio at NBBJ worked on the design of the Meany Hotel and the Gene Juarez Salon, both featured in this book.